P9-CCH-308

# BEING-IN,
# BEING-FOR,
# BEING-WITH

# BEING-IN, BEING-FOR, BEING-WITH

CLARK MOUSTAKAS, PH.D.

JASON ARONSON INC.
*Northvale, New Jersey*
*London*

Production Editor: Elaine Lindenblatt

This book was set in 11 pt. Palatino by Alpha Graphics of Pittsfield, New Hampshire, and printed and bound by Book-mart Press of North Bergen, New Jersey.

**Library of Congress Cataloging-in-Publication Data**

Moustakas, Clark E.
    Being-in, being-for, being-with / Clark Moustakas.
        p.  cm.
    Includes bibliographical references.
    ISBN 1-56821-537-1 (alk. paper)
    1. Individuality.   2. Self-actualization (Psychology)
3. Phenomenological psychology.   I. Title.
BF697.M667   1995
158—dc20                                        95-7080

Manufactured in the United States of America. Jason Aronson Inc. offers books and cassettes. For information and catalog write to Jason Aronson Inc., 230 Livingston Street, Northvale, New Jersey 07647.

For

Robert Moustakas

who is in, for, and with

creative photographic renditions of

nature, people, and life

# Contents

# Preface

This study has been taking shape over many years, most pointedly since the publication of my book *Creative Life* (Moustakas 1977a). Its themes have been dominant modes and structures of my way of being and relationships. They have provoked me into questions, doubts, probings, and reflections that at times opened channels of discovery that led to clarity and at other times left me puzzled, disturbed, restless, and silent.

The impetus for bringing *Being-In, Being-For, Being-With* to expression as a book was the desire to share a series of ideas, values, and meanings that have awakened within me during moments of peaceful self-reflection and in times of inner turbulence and restlessness. In my searches, I have attempted to arrive at an understanding of concepts of being, individuality, relationship, community, teaching and learning, loneliness, self-disclosure, and mystery.

My investigation of everyday challenges of being and relating has guided me into examining a series of pervasive themes: *being different*, its nature and meaning, its positive and negative associations; *creative process* and phenomenal discovery; *possessiveness* and being possessed; *power* and *control* in intimate relationships, *rhythms and rituals* in the development of trust, freedom, honesty, and will; and dimensions of *loneliness*, *mystery*, and *self-disclosure*.

I have often encountered root meanings in relationships, events, and conditions that enabled me to move beyond pain and alienation. I have understood more clearly the doubt and suffering that must be faced in coming to terms with betrayal; feelings and memories connected with old hurts, abuses, and rejections; and fears, shortcomings, and inadequacies aroused in moments of struggle, defeat, and failure.

A significant unfolding that emerged while creating this volume was the heightened awareness of the dialectical nature of freedom and boundaries—limits of freedom and an expanding sense of freedom within boundaries. I saw more clearly the issues, problems, tensions, and conflicts that arise when freedom and boundaries contend for supremacy in intimate relationships.

In thinking through the values and ideas that are explored in this volume, I saw that intimate contact with one's self makes possible intimate contact with others and that authentic and fundamental interaction with others enhances the meaning of privacy and solitude. I have realized too that paradoxically I am more free to be myself when others are free to be themselves. Thus, freedom of being depends on relationship, and relationship requires freedom of being. Ultimately, in the ideal, there is a synthesis of being and relating, a communion of self and other.

Looking specifically to the unfolding material presented in this volume, Chapter 1 introduces the firebrand, offers illustrations, presents firebrand activities, and details the significance of life as a firebrand.

Chapter 2 explores heuristic process in self-understanding and elucidates heuristic methods in science and personal-professional development.

Chapter 3 considers phenomenological methods of discovery of knowledge and the importance of language in fulfilling possibilities for growth.

Chapter 4 probes the nature of conventional thinking versus meditative thinking and presents the relationship between thinking and being.

Chapter 5 examines root meanings of relationship in terms of autobiographical connections, essential requirements of repetition and suffering in going through a stalemated relationship, and the therapeutic values of receptivity, attunement, and bodying forth. It also incorporates the values of Being-*In*, -*With*, and -*For* oneself and others in the development of significant relationships.

Chapter 6 invites an immersion into freedom and boundaries, an exploration of the nature and essences of these as contrasting values in relationships. Examples are presented of freedom without boundaries and freedom with boundaries as inherent in a shared life. Also explored in this chapter are solitude and boundaries, and community and boundaries, with a specific focus on the patterns that distinguish genuine existence from a life of unfulfilled promises. An additional emphasis of the chapter is the delineation of the "right to choose" contrasted with the making of a "good choice."

Chapter 7 contrasts possessing and being and discusses their meanings—the disguises of possessiveness, the rituals of being, and the search for authenticity in relationships.

Chapter 8 examines the dialectics of teaching and learning, how these processes work together in creating meanings and how they remain as separate entities in evoking distance and competition. As part of the dialectical search, "what teaching is" and "what learning is" are clarified from the point of view of the experiencing person.

Chapter 9 considers ways of intervening and anticipatory caring in relationships with children and how caring facilitates resolution of problems in therapy and in life.

Chapter 10 explores loneliness, mystery, and self-disclosure. Loneliness is viewed with reference to unfinished issues, in connection with solitude, and as an opening to new relationships. Also examined is mystery and self-disclosure, the mystery of the unfinished and unsettled, and the mystery of birth.

The final chapter presents a new model of psychotherapy, developed from my studies of phenomenology and my work as a human science researcher and psychotherapist, internship supervisor, and educator.

Having briefly described the basic themes of the individual chapters, I will now comment on how these themes originated, the process through which they were created, how they connect with each other, and their essential relationship to my own being.

For some time, I have been interested in themes of "being and relating" in my studies and experiences in philosophy, psychology, education, and psychotherapy. The nature of the self-discovery process has been a growing awareness over extended periods of isolation and solitude. Recently, I have awakened each morning and entered into a quiet, silent darkness. I have been attuned to inner states, seeking a life of openness and receptiveness and often achieving a purity of self-presence. I have become alert to what is within me, responding to movements in thought, feeling, and spirit.

Following a period of meditation, I experience an emptiness of being, an unusual and distinctive presence. In this state, a language begins to form, ways of Being-In, Being-For, and Being-With myself and others. Questions emerge on the nature and meaning of being and relating. In what ways do I express being? What thoughts and feelings, what spiritual and autobiographical connections, capture the essence of being? What is relationship? How does relationship affect my solitude? How do being and relating connect? What enables being within relationship? And relationship within being?

In my waking life, I accept what appears in my consciousness. I work in a way that honors my perceptions, meanings, and views. I flow with internal visions in creating awarenesses, understandings, judgments, and imaginative visions. My writing unfolds naturally, spontaneously, dedicated to a phenomenological process through which personal ideas, concepts, and meanings are constructed.

Each of the ideas in this volume is connected to my internal experience of time. Each evolved in the spaces of my being, an expanding presence that narrows in the face of darkness and pain and opens in episodes of levity and light. Each theme is connected bodily, awakening in an expansion and contraction of muscles, tissues, blood, and bones, a rising and falling of energy, the sense of flight, the pull of gravity. Each lives within a bodyhood that flows with the rise and fall of life itself. Each also connects texturally, in terms of feeling roots, passional qualities that awaken sensings and glimmerings, realities and fantasies. Each also holds a mystery and an invitation to solitude. Within these themes, there is the realization that life is generated from life, from living searches, from connections with others, from exemplary experiences, and from self-discoveries.

I have attempted to create an experiential language, to draw concepts out of internal meanings connected with personal and professional experience. I believe that these meanings will register and create a dialogue between speaker and audience.

# Acknowledgments

In the process of developing and completing *Being-In, Being-For, Being-With*, I have been to some degree enlightened by works of philosophy, psychology, education, literature, and human science. These are listed in the references pages of this volume. The writings of Paul Bridgman, Martin Heidegger, Michael Polanyi, and Carl Rogers have been particularly instructive in elucidating the nature of human behavior and experience, teaching and learning, creativity, the discovery of knowledge, and truth and intimacy in significant relationships. I have often been inspired to search more deeply, more uniquely, and more extensively by my students' questions and comments, and by the passionate, unfettered disclosures of their private worlds of loneliness and connectedness.

I express my appreciation to Kerry Moustakas for permission to quote extensively from her 1993 doctoral dissertation, "Encounters of Intimate Bonding: An Heuristic Investigation."

I also thank Cereta E. Perry, Ph.D., for permission to include her paper, "A Heuristic Search Through Self-Confrontation."

Credit is also owed for the inclusion in my book of a Rainer Maria Rilke poem from *The Book of Hours*.

My work on *Being-In, Being-For, Being-With* has been facilitated by Betty Moustakas in her creation of an atmosphere for writing and by rooms of silence and gentle spirits at the Center for Humanistic Studies.

I recognize Vange Puszcz in her typing of the entire manuscript through many changes and in her affirmations and Jill Benton, incomparable librarian, who is the best research detective I know for locating passages in long forgotten and sometimes obscure references and seeing that they are accurately recorded.

Clark Moustakas
March 17, 1995

# Introduction

*Being-In, Being-For, Being-With* has been created as a way of recognizing and affirming the nature and essence of Being and Relating, as well as mysteries of living and creative expressions of intimacy and power.

My intention is to lift out ideas and meanings from life experiences that hold individual and universal significance and that facilitate person-to-person interactions, connections that give birth to new awarenesses and encourage pathways to expression of feelings and values.

The aim is to evoke a human presence, a freedom to enter into peaks and valleys of experience, courage to walk through darknesses and traverse shadows of life itself. To achieve these aims, one must become internally alive, embrace one's own perceptions and senses, and face whatever appears in one's awareness and understanding—the imponderable and unknown regions of the self that inevitably occur in individual and communal living.

To *Be-In* means to cherish one's inner light, to stand out, as a unique being and to know others and life from the substance of one's own unique self.

To *Be-For* oneself requires that the person stand by her or his own values, convictions, and beliefs and not be swayed or manipulated by outside opinions, expectations, or demands. Being-For oneself means to support one's own creations and communications and to affirm one's own identity, one's feelings, one's choices and preferences. To Be-For is to confirm oneself. At no time does this have more immediate power and danger than when one is alone, on a private path, at a time when one is not being confirmed by anyone else. Being-For means daring to gaze inward and finding strength in self-resources and self-expressions. In Being-For oneself one remains with one's own perceptions and views; the evidence of one's own senses guides one in pursuit of the truth.

In Being-For oneself the person takes cues from the resources and possibilities of the self, from inner tendencies, leanings, interests, and tacit self-resources.

To *Be-With* oneself is a way of facing the polarities of one's world, a process of realizing that each contrasting component represents a legitimate voice and that the challenge is to find a place of harmony and balance among the diversity of possibilities and actualities, opposing views, inner tensions, and contrary ideas. To Be-With is a way of talking to oneself, of facing the fears and doubts of existence as well as the enticements and attractions of life, listening to the inner silences and words, and daring to cope with the strains of freedom and imprisonment. To Be-With is to accept and let be the forces of darkness and light, discovery and mystery, joy and sorrow, life and death.

*Being-In* oneself and *in* the world of others, *Being-For* oneself and *for* life, and *Being-With* oneself and *with* others are ways of being open to the possibilities of creative life, of being receptive to new rhythms, and of finding ways of expressing individuality, wholeness, and essence.

Truth in Being-In, -For, and -With becomes a form of self-other discovery, an heuristic process leading authentically to I and Thou. Each reality holds shapes and patterns and exists in its own terms; each leads to the freedom to explore regions of mind, heart, and soul or to be blocked by roles, rules, and expectations.

Freedom to be in truth becomes a passionate commitment, a process through which meanings are inherent in direct expressions of one's being. Such truth is born of unwavering integrity, devotion, and honesty, values that make available authentic resources and realities of Being-In, -For, and -With Oneself and Others.

Salman Rushdie (1992) emphasizes the imperative of holding on to one's own reality, to the truth and freedom of one's own self.

> Our lives teach us who we are. I have learned the hard way that when you permit anyone else's description of reality to supplant your own—and such descriptions have been raining down on me, from security advisers, governments, journalists, Archbishops, friends, enemies, mullahs—then you might as well be dead. Obviously, a rigid, blinkered, absolutist world view is the easiest to keep hold of, whereas the fluid, uncertain, metamorphic picture I've always carried is rather more vulnerable. Yet I must cling with all my might to my own soul; must hold on to its mischievous, iconoclastic, out-of-step clown instincts, no matter how great the storm. And if that plunges me into contradiction and paradox, so be it; I've lived in that messy ocean all my life. [p. 85]

**1**

# Firebrand:
# The Experience
# of Being Different

When I consider the transitions that have stood out in my development in recent years, I awaken to an acute awareness of the urgent need for freedom, autonomy, and self-direction in life and the threats to these values that surround us everywhere. Sometimes there is no other way but through direct confrontation with people who are manipulating and controlling our lives and whose aim is to deny, block, and restrain us from the freedom of being and from creative self-expression. Increasingly, I am discovering the imperative of facing people openly when the truth of my world is being ignored, denied, or altered to suit their needs and purposes.

People in high professional and political positions, people of power, are daily proclaiming the necessity and justification for restrictive regulations and programs, the fine measure of their purposes and goals. All the while, the world is threatened with extinction, the environment is increasingly polluted, and structures are collapsing. What "they" call growth is in reality something decaying, dying, or dead. What they call "entering a new era" is another form of darkness. In the mainstream of the everyday world, the breach between promise and actuality grows deeper and wider.

## CAROL: FAMILY FIREBRAND

A long time ago, Carol, a child I had been meeting with in play therapy, taught me how politics works in a family. She showed me how a person in authority might call something good that is actually harmful, might label something "enhancing" that is blemished and impure. I still remember that first day when Carol paced back and forth in the playroom, a proud, defiant little girl, determined to speak out on behalf of her own truth. She had learned a critical lesson of life. In the segment that follows, drawn from a significant hour with Carol, she refers to her mother , who regularly attempted to persuade her that what she offered her was in her best interests. "It's only for your own good, darling," she would say, and it always turned out to be rotten for Carol.

> "I have to shine my glasses", Carol would shout over and over again, in the playroom. "*Some* glasses she gave me. I'm gonna tell her this is no good. It's not even glass."
> "She gave you some pretty poor glasses?"
> "Now listen," Carol screamed, pointing her finger, "I want some good glasses." She pretended to open the new package. "Same old glasses."
> "She gives you rotten ones again. You've been cheated so many times."
> "Yes, they always look shining but they're no good."

Ultimately Carol prevailed as a distinctive person because she dared repeatedly to bring her own light into the family darkness. No matter how often her parents tried to convince her that what they told her was for her own good she knew that something was radically wrong with the way she was being treated in her family. Carol survived because she refused to eat the apple that her parents fed her.

Carol was the troublemaker in her family because she dared to question what she was being told. She knew she did not want or need what her parents insisted was best for her. She inflamed her parents by bringing her own being into their world, by daring to be the firebrand in her family, daring to stand by her own perceptions, judgments, and preferences, and daring to decide for herself what things are and mean. She constantly agitated them, mirrored their hypocrisy, and revealed their deceptiveness and dishonesty.

## DESCRIPTION OF THE FIREBRAND

The firebrand is the person who recognizes what is natural, what is organic, what is alive and vital in life, the person who dares to live, to be, and to create, often in the face of interference, rejection, deceit, and betrayal. The firebrand is a burning ember, life that is in each of us and that provides the spark and energy to speak against what distorts, hides, and denies our being and truth. It is that which awakens within us, when we must declare our independence or when we discover a new formula for living. It is the path that enables us to participate in the mystery of creation, uniquely and individually. The firebrand expresses her- or himself in two basic ways: as the torch that lights up the darkness, and as the carrier of the torch, throwing light into the darkness, and often disturbing complacency and brewing trouble. Being a firebrand is a way of raising temperatures and creating conflict, turbulence, and dissension.

The motive of the firebrand is not to attack or destroy others but to bring to light a basic truth, to take a stand, and to declare and own who one is, especially in the face of perceived violations of one's values and rights and interferences with one's goals, purposes, and meanings.

In relation to one's self, the firebrand engages in reflection and self-dialogue that evokes awareness of ideas, projects, and goals, insights into one's deviance from others, and particularly from mainstream people. The firebrand chooses to be different when being different represents a truth, when being different guides the fulfillment of basic human values and actualization of one's potentials.

In relation to others, the firebrand seeks to maintain what is unique and distinctive, what will enrich a relationship and keep it alive in fundamental ways. The firebrand avoids roles, categories, classifications, hierarchies, fixed routines, and practices but rather seeks to create rituals, searches for new rhythms and connections with others, keeps secrets and confidences, and engages in conflicts and intimacies when these are true to experience, when these are ways of enhancing life. The firebrand is concerned with being open, honest, adventurous, and creative. If none of these processes are viable, the firebrand terminates the activity or relationship and moves on.

## FIREBRAND ACTIVITIES

When we engage in firebrand activities, the power of our own inner light sustains us through difficult times. I share briefly a list of major firebrand events that enabled me to grow personally and professionally.

1. I was determined to do qualitative research at a university that approved only quantitative designs in doctoral programs. I committed myself to an investigation of the nature and meaning of children's learning experiences in different socioeconomic settings. I believed that I could obtain this knowledge validly only through participant observations in the settings where children lived and learned. I was convinced that I could understand personality expres-

sion through communications and descriptions that came directly from the child participants. This put me at odds with my professors, who were unyielding and exclusively committed to quantitative research. Their opposition opened up between us many struggles, tensions, and conflicts. In spite of their threats regarding my status as a student, I persisted in what I believed to be a significant research project.

2. From the beginning of my work with children, I saw that, at times, only unconditional love and belief in the child's potentials for growth would rescue the child from a deteriorating self-image and destructive environment. This often meant affirming whatever the child expressed, the deviant and peculiar in the child, especially when others were treating the child's uniqueness as a sickness. My stand created considerable conflict with other professionals, with colleagues, and, at times, with parents and teachers. The outcome of these confrontations, observations, studies, and experiences was a series of publications on teaching and learning—*The Young Child in School* (with Minnie P. Berson; 1956), *The Teacher and the Child* (1956c), *The Authentic Teacher* (1966a), *Teaching as Learning* (1972b), *Learning to Be Free* (with Cereta E. Perry; 1973), and *Who Will Listen? Children and Parents in Therapy* (1975b).

3. I met all children in therapy at a school where I was employed—in opposition to the administrators of the psychological clinic. I believed that I could learn a great deal about pathology from healthy children and much about health from children labeled as emotionally disturbed, autistic, or mentally retarded. This made no sense to my supervisors. I was criticized, judged, attacked, and threatened with dismissal. Accounts of my work with a wide range of children in therapy (based on observation, tape-recorded interviews, and reflective analyses) were published in a series of books, including *Children in Play Therapy: A Key to Under-*

*standing Normal and Disturbed Emotions* (1953), *Psychotherapy with Children* (1956a), *Existential Child Therapy* (editor) (1966b), and *Rhythms, Rituals and Relationships* (1981).

4. I opposed institutionalization of children many, many years ago when institutionalization was virtually automatic in cases of autism, mental retardation, and extreme withdrawal or hostility states. This put me in jeopardy with psychiatrists, social workers, psychologists, and educators, and in some instances with parents who insisted on hospitalization. Case presentations, analyses, and follow-up studies are included in the previously listed titles and in the values, principles, theories, and social meanings and implications grounded in observation and experience, outlined and discussed in my publications *Creativity and Conformity* (1967), *Individuality and Encounter* (1968), *Turning Points* (1977b), and *Creative Life* (1977a).

5. In my very first work in public schools, I encouraged teachers to develop relationships with children to focus on the feelings inherent in language, to be concerned with creativity, to permit freedom of choice in learning. This resulted in considerable dissension and difficulty with some principals and with the superintendent of the school district who attempted to fire me from the university that employed me. My university colleagues considered my behavior foolhardy, risky, and wasteful of time, energy, and resources.

From these first ventures in graduate education and in professional work I identified myself as a firebrand, in the sense of D. H. Lawrence (1961):

> Yea and no man dared even throw a firebrand into the darkness. For if he did he was jeered to death by the others, who cried "Fool, anti-social knave, why would you disturb us with bogeys? There *is* no darkness. We move and live and have our being within the light, and unto us is given the eternal light of knowledge. Fool and knave, how dare you belittle us with the darkness?" [pp. 437–438]

This volume is to some degree an outcome of my awakening to the significance of the firebrand in families, schools, and society. During the past eight years, a major firebrand project has been my activities with and encouragement of graduates of alternative psychology programs to revolt against violations of their constitutional rights and conspiracies aimed at freedom to compete and practice one's profession, while supporting the wisdom of choosing for oneself the most effective education and training in psychology, congruent with one's own philosophy of learning, values, purposes, and interests. I have taken an unwavering and persistent stand against national associations and boards of psychology who encroach on academic freedom, prescribe courses and titles, homogenize the curriculum, and in other ways tamper with the unique missions and purposes of graduate schools and programs in psychology that emphasize individuality, diversification, interdisciplinary studies, and applications that are socially relevant and that contribute directly to enhancing the lives and well-being of all people in the community and in the world. The firebrand opposes discrimination of every kind, including that which appears under the guise of professional competency, role power, and protection of the public—too often this translates into guild interests, promotion of the in-group and rules, criteria, and doctrines that exclude and limit people who embrace different theories, values, views, and beliefs and who are qualified and competent to do professional work congruent with their education, knowledge, and experience.

6.  Betty, my wife, and I remained with Kerry, our daughter, throughout her open heart surgery, at a time when, and in a hospital where, parents were excluded except during limited visiting hours. This resulted in strong and tense discussions and frequent battles with the medical staff. They wanted us out of the way, but we refused to leave. I believe

that our decision to remain with Kerry ultimately saved her life. Being at the hospital continuously over a period of weeks opened my eyes to the nature of loneliness, to what happens to young children when they are abandoned by their parents and turned over to strangers who put them through frightening and painful procedures. I witnessed the shift in hospitalized children from assertiveness and protest to fear and despair, and eventually to a state of chronic depression. As with Kerry, the very life of some children was at stake. The hospital was a place that could kill as well as cure. Several children died following their open heart surgery, because of the negligence of medical staff and the absence of caretakers. From these studies of children and families in hospital settings and in therapy, I completed a series of heuristic works, including *Loneliness* (1961), *Loneliness and Love* (1972a), *Portraits of Loneliness and Love* (1974b), and *The Touch of Loneliness* (1975a).

7. More than thirty years ago, I helped found a new psychology that would recognize the person, as a whole human being, with potentials for life and growth, that would value the internal frame of reference and self-experience as fundamental and valid ways to knowledge and truth. Participation in the founding of the Association for Humanistic Psychology put me into considerable conflict with my behavioral and psychoanalytic colleagues and resulted in my being attacked for several years at virtually every gathering of psychologists and mental health workers. With assistance from A. H. Maslow, Dorothy Lee, Carl R. Rogers, Ross L. Mooney, Gordon W. Allport, David Smillie, Frances Wilson, Sita Ram Jayaswal, and others, I edited a book entitled *The Self: Explorations in Personal Growth* (1956b), which helped launch the humanistic psychology movement and made legitimate studies of loneliness, love, autonomy, individuality, being and becoming, creativity, the healthy personality, the person in psychology, self-actualization,

and a range of topics and questions relevant to human nature, human beings, human processes, and human behavior and experience.

The Association for Humanistic Psychology, and colleagues whom I had met and worked with since its founding in 1958, encouraged me to pursue studies that had not been included or supported in conventional psychology. These included *Personal Growth: The Struggle for Identity and Human Values* (1969), and *Finding Yourself, Finding Others* (1974a), as well as many of the titles listed earlier.

8. I helped establish a new graduate school, a nonconventional residential school rooted in phenomenology, existentialism, humanistic psychology, and qualitative studies of human experience, when the voices around told me that such ventures were bound to fail and that my family and I would suffer from continual frustrations, pressures, and losses. The school, the Center for Humanistic Studies in Detroit, is regionally accredited and has full enrollments each year and a substantial endowment to ensure its continuity and longevity. The outlook is optimistic and solid for this graduate school in psychology to grow and become an even more effective and resourceful center for the creative education and training of humanistic psychologists and for contributions in education and health care services. An important stream of study and activity of the Center for Humanistic Studies is the research projects based on human science inquiry and qualitative designs and methodology that have been completed by the graduates and faculty of the center as well as applications of existential, phenomenological, and heuristic models of psychotherapy to clinical practice. Some of these research studies and applications to therapy are outlined and described in my books *Phenomenology, Science, and Psychotherapy* (1988), *Heuristic Research: Design, Methodology and Applications* (1990), and *Phenomenological Research Methods* (1994a).

These firebrand activities have enabled me to continue to develop as an individual and to use my deviation from the norm as an opportunity for learning. The firebrand awakens in me the desire and the power to speak, to write, and to create. Virtually all the events of my firebrand nature have at times aroused others to name calling, abusive language, and both subtle and overt attacks. The most common charge has been that I desire to gain power and control over others. I know the difference between the power of being and knowledge, "personal-professional power," and that of role and politics. I have been warned and threatened, but somehow I have persisted in holding onto my beliefs and values. I have continued to discover ways to significant growth for myself and support of others. At times only my own will, and my own strength, courage, and knowledge, affirmed me and enabled me to continue to live in situations of intense attack aimed at bringing about my conformity or reducing me to passive silence.

One may carry a torch and awaken people without creating turmoil and disturbance. Terry Fox, the young Canadian who walked across Canada, was a firebrand. He lit up the entire country of Canada and awakened a unity among people in the fight to conquer cancer. He aroused a nation to respond affirmatively to people with disabilities everywhere.

Above all else, the firebrand is true to what is alive, to what is burning within, to the callings of life and the imperative of speaking out on behalf of individual and human rights.

The firebrand is a distinctive individual who responds to inner commands that will haunt the person until she or he recognizes, proclaims, and pursues them. In the words of Jung (1957):

Hence it is not the universal and the regular that characterize the individual, but rather the unique. He is not to be understood as a recurrent unit but as something unique and singular which in the last analysis can neither be known nor compared with anything else. (pp. 17–18)

## HEURISTIC MEANING AND INDIVIDUALITY

Long ago St. Bonaventure explained that there are three kinds of knowledge: "The Eye of the Flesh," which comes from direct sense experience; "The Eye of Reason," knowledge not directly observable but derived through cognitive steps; and "The Eye of Contemplation," which dwells inside one's self in spiritual meanings and discloses to one's self absolute realities.

To these three eyes, I add the "heuristic" eye, which is an eye of its own and does not belong to any category. To be heuristic means to discover through one's own internal awareness and intuition. It is this eye that we must hold onto to maintain our individuality, the eye from which we feel and know the nature and meaning of our own experience, what is true of our life. The heuristic is intuitive and personal and represents the truth of our own experience, our own becoming nature. The heuristic is the eye from which the fires of being arise. Its opposite is publicness—the passing off or sale of ourselves as familiar, the way of adjusting and adapting to others' interests and expectations, a way of becoming accessible to everyone.

Distance, averageness, and leveling down are qualities of publicness, the "They" in Heidegger's (1962) terms. And *They* are always right, not because *They* are distinctive and primary, not because of their actual relation to the truth of things, but because *They* are in positions of power; they know what is right; they use their roles and status to direct and control us. *They* are insensitive to every difference, to every act of genuineness. *They* never get to the heart of the matter, caught up as *They* are in the surface of things and in rules that reflect their own fears and their need to manipulate and control others.

In such social and political systems, everyone is the other and no one is an authentic self. Full appreciation of the process of recognizing individuality focuses on awareness and understanding of oneself. To value oneself, one must value what is within, savoring it, soaking it up, coming to terms with it, rather than classifying, judging, and evaluating it. The heuristic focuses on the inner truth of *being with* one's own values and meanings. In such moments, the individual is patient and permits *what is* to be, to linger and endure. Being patient means that what exists as authentic has its own timetable, recognizes that growth is an unfolding process and that new forms emerge through a readiness, a gradual opening and awakening, and through reflective consideration.

When we value individuality, we respect the right of people to direct their lives, to experience feelings in their own way, to discover their own unique pathways and meanings in life.

Bill put it this way: "I'm going to therapy because my teacher says I have a problem. I'm a hyperactive child." But what does it mean to be hyperactive? For Bill, being hyperactive meant having "wild, powerful animals inside me that are screaming to get out. I have to move. I have to move." And so move he did. He settled into ferocious rhythms, exaggerated jumps and leaps, extreme forms of being in the world—until all the wild animals were out roaming and he would sit quietly and draw or read or work in his own way. He could contain the wild creatures only so long and then they had to come out. Bill was rooted to his inner fury; he brooded with it, lingered inside of it until by its very nature he had to break out into the open, explode into wild gestures and grand movements.

Bill's experience is that of the firebrand, not different in essence from Archimedes's experience. While bathing Archimedes suddenly understood a new principle of buoyancy. He ran naked through the streets shouting, "I have found it.

I have found it." Bill found *it* too in permitting his wild inner animals to roam freely in grand external movements and thus discovering peacefulness, harmony, and balance in his life.

This is precisely what happens in the honoring of individuality. One discovers what one has been searching to know. In the process, there is often a sudden burst of meaning that leads to an intense, pure state, a joy in recognition, a light of knowledge or understanding that helps one embrace one's own ideas and feelings. Thomas de Hartman (1972) expresses this quality in emphasizing that the interior world contains the seed in which art awakens and takes root. The interior region of the self is the magic part of life, without which there would be no poetry, or music, or rhythm, or soul.

The denial of individuality is itself the problem; it forces one to become deviant or to fight to keep alive one's uniqueness and requires the use of vital energies to protect oneself. Or, it leads to the surrendering of oneself to the demands of others, thus the giving up of one's own source of energy and power. The turning over of one's self to someone else undermines decision making, health, and well-being.

Long ago, Otto Rank (1950) stated:

> Psychologically the problem of individuality is a will problem and consciousness problem. The neurotic character represents not illness but a developmental phase of the individuality problem, a personality denying its own will, not accepting itself as an individual. . . . [T]he neurotic type represents the individual knowing about himself . . . but repressing this knowledge, not wanting to be conscious of himself. [p. 221]

The individuality of behavior should be recognized for what it is—simply behavior that is different. In encouraging the expression of individuality, we look for signs of agitation that will support people in breaking out of their prisons, in shining forth as human beings.

My therapy sessions with Tony were filled with witches, ghosts, and demons who eventually were revealed as his mother and teacher, people who attempted to manipulate and mold him and who were constantly frustrated and defeated by his peculiar ways. He found his own way with people who attempted to control him. He was skillful in using clairvoyance to cope with others' expectations and demands. With a mix of magic, precognition, and chanting, he would totally confuse the adults in his life. To them, he appeared "dumb," "slow-witted," "strange," and "dull." He kept them off balance with his wizardry. He kept them out of sync with imaginative expressions. In this way, he protected himself from rejection and attack. He was not in touch with what they called the real world. By appearing "slow" to them, he was easily dismissed as retarded. They left him alone since he had little to offer.

In therapy with me, however, he was a glorious and inventive child. I became completely fascinated and involved in his "experiments." They opened new doors for both of us. We read materials ranging from parapsychology and transpersonal reports to chemistry manuals, at the very time that he was in a slow, "preprimer" reading group in school. We created magical moments and conducted a variety of compelling experiments. Eventually Tony's teacher and mother discovered that his peculiarity, strangeness, and slow, reluctant expressions were not a form of retardation but rather expressions of a unique and individual way of being. As his therapist, I recognized this vital force in Tony, his special energy and talents. I offered him, in words and actions, a life that encouraged the magic that was within him to shine forth. I found resources that would challenge and extend his learning in the areas of his interests.

To enter fully into understanding the experience of being different, one must listen to oneself, to the voices within that have been silent or muted and that clamor to be heard. Daniel Levinson (1977), in his study of midlife transitions, describes what the process is like:

> He may hear only a vague whispering, the content unclear but the tone indicating grief over lost opportunities, outrage over betrayal by others, or guilt over betrayal by himself. Or the voices may come through as a thunderous roar, the content all too clear, stating names and times and places and demanding that something be done to right the balance. He hears the voice of an identity prematurely rejected; of a love lost or not pursued; of a valued interest or relationship given up in aquiescence to parental or other authorities; of an internal figure who wants to be an athlete or nomad or artist. . . . [H]e must learn to listen more attentively to these voices and in the end, to decide what part he will give them in his life. [p. 108]

The renewal of contact with one's self, the declaration of one's independence, the honoring of one's individuality are what enables a return to freedom, authenticity, and a sense of power over one's own fate and destiny. The birth of individuality is a source of energy and life that can be the basis for exploring, experimenting, and knowing, a realization that the essence of selfhood is uniqueness and that ultimately one can only experience what is one's own, from one's own organism, that in each instance the verdict of meaning and relevance must come from the texture and structure of one's own experiencing and a felt bodily sense that speaks to what is actual. Acceptance of the experience of being different enables one to reach a heightened state of awareness of the important facets of one's world, the nature of feelings, the significance of people, how the constituents of one's world affect one's perceptions. Being different is a way of discovering one's self and others, a way of knowing what distinguishes wheat from chaff, what nourishes and satisfies, what uplifts and supports. Being different is not a fixed or permanent state but is affected by the currents of everyday living, by the growing clarity of what matters, who to trust, and how to live.

Alex, at age 8, had lost the wildness of his world, the uniqueness and life of childhood. And yet something strong lingered, something compelling drew him unto himself.

> [M]emories would come on wings of light—shining bird, high pines and sun, the fire in a floating leaf, the autumn heat in weathered wood . . . soft lichen on a stone—a light filled imminence, shimmering and breathing, and yet so fleeting that it left him breathless and in pain. [Mathiessen, 1978, p. 42]

This sense of contact with the real life within one's self is what the firebrand seeks to maintain. As a firebrand, in the determination to grow, there will be moments when the only genuine act is to toss the burning embers of one's heart and soul into the deadwood; to burn a path to creative thinking; to protest against corruption and irresponsibility; to turn on a light that exposes discrimination and injustice; to take a stand wherever people are excluding or controlling others, stifling their individuality, and threatening to destroy unique and original sources of life.

## CONCLUDING COMMENTS

Although I am emphasizing the imperative of the commitment to be alert to the violations of what it means to be an individual human being and to be politically active, I do not want to lose touch with the other side—the imperative of one's own privacy and the life of solitude. Whatever else, we must save something for ourselves and never become just instruments for programs of others, however important they may be.

We must make sure that some part of our life is kept alive, reserved for us and that no one or nothing else substitutes for this value. Regardless of how much pulling and tugging we must do on behalf of others or political and professional goals, we must not lose touch with the sacred spirit that is in each of us. We must keep that alive in moments of discovery, meditation, and self-dialogue. We must hold onto that which is distinctly our own, that unique and lonely center that forever seeks its own presence, recognition, and expression. In the midst of outside callings and needs, we must continue to reserve a place for ourselves, to make time and space for knowing the essence of who we are as individuals, the deep and abiding core, that is now, that is growing, that is forever.

**2**

---

# The Heuristic Process
# in Discovery
# of Knowledge

Heuristic discovery of knowledge is an inward journey, an unconditional commitment to deepening and extending personal knowledge that is embedded in universal meanings. The process is launched by questions and concerns that inspire self-awareness, self-dialogues, and self-explorations.

Heuristic research is an approach to scientific study that employs methods and processes aimed at illuminating the nature of a phenomenon and seeking its explication. In this regard, Polanyi (1969) observed that "vague shapes of the surmised truth suddenly take on sharp outlines of certainty only to dissolve again in the light of second thoughts. Yet from time to time certain visions of the truth, having made their appearance, continue to gain strength both by further reflection and additional evidence" (p. 30).

Heuristic meanings came into my life when I was searching for a word that would meaningfully encompass the processes that I believed to be essential in investigations of human experience. At the time, I was engaged in studies of loneliness. The root meaning of *heuristic* comes from the Greek word *heuriskein*, to discover or to find. It refers to a process of internal search through which one discovers the nature and meaning of experience and develops methods and procedures for further investigation and analysis. The researcher is present as a person throughout the process and, through internal search and self-dialogue, comes to understand the phenomenon with increasing depth. Heuristic processes in themselves open possibilities for new directions in one's life (Moustakas 1990).

The heuristic investigation may be viewed as a labyrinth containing myriad pathways that challenge, distress, confuse, fascinate, and puzzle the researcher. In such searches, we often seek renewal in meanings that transcend restrictive thoughts and that move us forward in our thirst for new knowledge.

Ellen Dooling Draper (1992) comments:

> Throughout the history of humankind, the labyrinth appears and reappears in many different variations.... [Y]et the symbol contains more than just a puzzle to be solved. The way of the hero . . . goes beyond the search for an answer, beyond the solution of the maze, on the road to his or her destiny; the hero in each of us seeks the challenge of the unknown and welcomes the incomprehensible and the threatening, for it is through the mystery and the danger that new avenues are opened up. The labyrinth can be seen as an emblem of transformation, a kind of roadmap towards a new possibility. [pp. 2–3]

Being lost occurs in the initial phase of the heuristic journey and includes the determination and will to explore the maze and find one's way through the levels and realms of meaning that circumscribe and illuminate one's own experience. Such a process might simply be dismissed as old-fashioned solipsism, but if the heuristic search is a type of solipsism, it is not the private solipsism of traditional philosophy. It is a way of self-engagement and self-dialogue, but it is also rooted in meanings that have a universal application. The most personal truths hold a general significance. In *Wittgenstein—The Later Philosophy*, Finch (1977) emphasized that the traditional solipsist did not go far enough but stopped halfway in the analysis. The old-fashioned solipsist imprisoned self-searching and made it a self-encased, private phenomenon. The traditional solipsist did not see the way out into the world. Wittgenstein informs us:

> [w]hat is correct in solipsism . . . and the Cartesian privacy . . . but an incommunicability which is . . . *wholly public* . . . not because the I is private, or this first person experience is private . . . [but] because of the nature of language . . . the "first person world" and "the first person experience" . . . *do not belong to anybody*, but are, rather overwhelming public. [p. 106]

In *Philosophical Investigations*, Wittgenstein (1953) observed that the aim of philosophy is to show the fly the way out of the fly bottle or, put in another way, to propel the first-person experience into an openness that is absolutely unique and at the same time absolutely worldly.

In this sense, the heuristic search is akin to the enlightenment of Satori. Onda (1972) describes the process:

> It is comparable to vividly experiencing personally coldness of water and heat of fire. It is an experience into which the self and the object are integrated. . . . When the [Zen] trainee leaves the mental state in which he [or she] has seen the outer world as the object of the self, and enters the state in which . . . self and outer world unite into one, the fixed view-point changes completely and new ideas arise freely. [p. 588]

Dilthey (1976) also emphasizes the unity of knowledge between self and world. He asserts:

To the perceiving mind the external world remains only a phenomenon but to the whole human being who wills, feels, and imagines, this external reality . . . is something independent and as immediately given and certain as his [or her] own self—it is part of life, not a mere idea. We do not know this external world through an inference from effects to causes or some corresponding process; the ideas of cause and effect are only abstractions from the life of the will. Thus, the horizon of experience widens: at first it only seems to tell us about our own inner states but in knowing myself I also know about the external world and other people. [p. 162]

In a similar vein of meaning, Matsuo Basho contributes this aphorism:

You can learn about the pine only from the pine, or about bamboo only from bamboo. When you see an object, you must leave your subjective preoccupation with yourself; otherwise you impose yourself on the object, and do not learn. The object and yourself must become one, and from that feeling of oneness issues your poetry. However well phrased it may be, if your feeling is not natural—if the object and yourself are separate—then your poetry is not true poetry but merely your subjective counterfeit.

When I consider an issue, problem, or question heuristically, I focus on what is immediately present in my conscious awareness, on just what stands out. I enter into meditative reflections that are alive with possibilities and meanings. I receive, accept, support, and encourage what is there, allow it to awaken fully. I let it be and, in the letting be, create a clearing that advances my understanding and makes knowing possible. The process is one that allows me to remain an individual while also related to others and life.

For example, I have asked myself, "What does it mean to know another person?" The answer came in periods of self-reflection as I considered my life with children and adults with whom I was meeting in therapy. To really know another person in significant moments of that person's life, I listen to

> the range of voices, the variations of speech, the tones and textures, sounds of joy and anger, the mixture of sadness and laughter, the edgy, uncertain words of fear, the myriad facial and body expressions—surprise, doubt, shock, terror, rage, madness—the lengthy silences and continuous stream of words that seem never to stop coming, and all the ups and downs of ecstasy and misery. [Moustakas 1975b, p. xi]

I listen purely to understand the meaning of those flat, empty sounds and those cold, vacant, almost frozen stares. I listen to the "contradictions of inner and outer forces that create an agonizing conflict in which courage is a disguised form of fear, kindness is actually dishonesty, laughter covers tears and sweetness is a form of rage" (Moustakas 1975b, p. xi).

> To fully know another person is a long journey of listening, feeling, sensing, risking, trusting, doubting, joining, wandering alone, confronting, loving, supporting, opposing, laughing, weeping. When two people actually meet and create a full life, a sense of mutuality is present; each is alive and responsive to the other. The vibrations are unlike any others. Such a relationship follows a unique path, without tangible or predictable directions, without prescribed rules and regulations. The essence of such a relationship is a mystery, happening but once and unrepeatable. . . . Each moment with another human being represents an opportunity for discovery and birth, or for confusion and destruction. Each moment holds the potential for life or death. I have chosen to infuse my spirit into each venture with a child or adult, to risk my own self in the hope of knowing the glory of a voice that speaks for the first time, of recognizing the birth of individuality, of seeing dead energy and spirit suddenly emerging into new forms and activities and sparking a light that radiates out of the darkness. [Moustakas 1975b, pp. xi-xii]

I have emphasized (Moustakas 1990) that in the discovery process, I am often entranced by visions and images of knowing and being that connect me to my self and others. When I remain focused on my experience, I find myself drawing up to it. I dwell inside it.

In my efforts to understand human experience, I have recognized six phases of the heuristic process. The first phase I have called *the initial engagement* in which I discover a question that holds a compelling interest for me, perhaps a problem that has involved me personally and that has awakened in me a passionate and determined commitment to grapple with it until I find some answer or resolution. The initial engagement involves self-dialogue, encounters with one's own self, and inward searches and inquiries that will help clarify the problem and expand knowledge of it.

Once I have developed sufficient clarification of my issue, question, or problem, I am ready to immerse myself in it completely.

The second phase of the heuristic process I have called *immersion*. During this phase I am seized with determination to discover knowledge on an issue, problem, or question. I am alive with energy and purpose. I want to live my question and grow in knowledge and understanding of it. I immerse myself completely in it. For a while it is the center of my world. My question follows me around. Even in my sleep, it is the center of my dreams. In waking life, my eyes are open. My ears are alert for any reference to it. Conversations, books, newspapers, lectures, anything whatever that relates to my search becomes raw material from which I seek clues, facts, meanings that will contribute to my knowledge.

When my life has been completely saturated with my search to discover the nature and meaning of an issue or problem, I find myself growing weary and feeling exhausted. I have stretched my energies and resources to the limit. I need a period of rest. This period initiates the next phase of heuristic discovery—the *incubation* phase. I am no longer directly preoccupied by my question or problem. A seed has been firmly planted. It undergoes silent nourishment and care, which allows for inward creative resources to emerge, take hold, and burst through to a deepening and extending of my understanding. On a conscious level, I am engrossed in entirely different matters but within me is a growing awareness or knowing and involvement, an active inner life that increasingly contributes to my understanding.

Polanyi (1964) asserts that discovery does not ordinarily occur through deliberate mental operations and calculated efforts to reach a mountain peak "but more often comes in a flash after a period of rest or distraction. Our labors are spent as it were in an unsuccessful scramble among the rocks. . . . [W]hen we would give up for a moment and settle down to tea we suddenly find ourselves transported to the top . . . by a process of spontaneous mental reorganization uncontrolled by conscious effort" (p. 34).

This kind of discovery of a new path I have called *illumination*, the fourth phase of heuristic research. Illumination occurs spontaneously. It is a birth process, an awakening, when all at once I understand or see something I have not understood or seen before. I have uncovered meanings that significantly alter my perception of reality. Illumination opens the door to a new awareness that moves the searcher importantly to the answer to a question or resolution of a problem.

I remember how often I have passed a place without noticing something crucial for my own direction, such as when I am lost in a city and go around and around, each time missing what I am looking for. Then just when I decide to simply enjoy being lost, suddenly I recognize a familiar store, school, or some landmark, and I easily find my way out of the maze. How often I have looked for something I had misplaced, like a key, an important document, or my glasses. The more deliberately and actively I try to remember or search for it, the more frustrated I become. When I stop looking and become involved in something else, typically I experience a flash and then a vision of the thing, and I know exactly where to find it.

In illumination, it is just such missed or distorted memories and realities that make their appearance with clarity and add something essential to our knowledge.

Once I have experienced the illumination of discovery, I am ready to engage my question or problem in a new way. I call this next phase the *explication process*. I understand something more tangible, more substantive, more illuminated. I need to deepen and expand my knowledge for full clarification of a question or resolution of a problem. I examine further what has awakened in my consciousness. I recognize new constituencies, new angles, new perspectives and views relevant to my search. I dwell inside the question from the vantage point of an increased understanding. I explicate each of the components or themes that underlie and characterize the question or problem until a comprehensive understanding of the components is achieved. The angles, textures, features are articulated. Refinements and corrections are made. I am now ready to enter the final phase of the heuristic discovery of knowledge—the *creative synthesis*.

Having mastered knowledge of the parts, the challenge is to organize the major components, as such and in their interconnectedness, to put them together into a whole. To develop a creative synthesis, I allow my intuition and tacit awareness to take hold in such a way that I am able to move beyond the constriction of parts and synthesize them into a wholeness that in essence and meaning answers my question or leads to the resolution of my problem.

For me, the discovery of heuristic processes as a basis for search and inquiry, leading to deepening and expanding of knowledge, began with my studies of loneliness (Moustakas 1961, 1972, 1975). As I recounted in my book *Heuristic Research* (1990), I set out to discover the meaning of loneliness in its simplest terms and in its native state. I knew from my

own experiences and from my conversations with hospitalized children that loneliness itself could not be communicated by words or defined in its essence, or appreciated and
reorganized except by persons who are open to their own
senses and aware of their own experiences. I set out to discover the nature of lonely experience by intimate encounter
with other persons, and with the understanding that "into
every act of knowing there enters a tacit and passionate con-
tribution of the person knowing what is being known, and
that this coefficient is no mere imperfection, but a vital component of all knowledge" (Polanyi 1958, p. 312).

Initially, I studied loneliness in its essential forms by putting myself into an open, ready state, into the lonely experiences of hospitalized children, and letting these experiences
become the focus of my world. . . . In dialogue with the children, I tried to put into words the depth of their feelings. Sometimes my words touched a child and tears began to flow; sometimes the child formed words in response to my presence, and
broke through the numbness and the dehumanizing impact
of the hospital atmosphere and practice. In a strong sense,
loneliness became my existence. . . . Without reference to time
or place or structure, somehow (more intentionally than acci-
dentally) the loneliness theme came up everywhere in my life.
. . . I was totally immersed in the search for a pattern that
would reveal the various dimensions of loneliness. I was in-
quiring into the nature of a human experience, not from a
detached intellectual or academic position, but in its integra-
tive, living forms. I had, at moments, gone "wide open"—
ceasing to be a separate individual, but wholly related to the
other person, leaving something behind of my own intuitive
vision and comprehension while at the same time taking
something away—very much in the manner of Steinbeck and
Ricketts (1941) in their study of the *Sea of Cortez*:

> Let's see what we see, record what we find, and not only fool
> ourselves with conventional scientific strictures—in that

lonely and uninhabited Gulf our boat and ourselves would
change it the moment we entered. By going there, we would
bring a new factor to the Gulf. Let us consider that factor and
not be betrayed by this myth of permanent reality. If it exists
at all it is only available in pickled tatters or in distorted
flashes. "Let us go," we said, "into the Sea of Cortez, realizing that we become forever a part of it; that our rubber boots
slogging through a flat of eelgrass, that the rocks we turn over
in a tide pool, make us truly and permanently a factor in the
ecology of the region. We shall take something away from it,
but we shall leave something too." [p. 3]

In a similar way, I began a formal study of loneliness. . . . I
steeped myself in a world of loneliness, letting my life take
root and unfold in it, letting its dimensions and meanings and
forms evolve in its own timetable and dynamics and ways.

## AN HEURISTIC SEARCH
## THROUGH SELF-CONFRONTATION

My colleague and friend, Cereta Perry, recently entered into
a heuristic process in an effort to understand what was
happening in one of her classes and how to change its
destructive effects. Here is an account of her heuristic self-
confrontation.

"The process began after I had read student evaluations.
During periods of reflection, I focused on feelings of discom-
fort that I experienced in four consecutive class meetings. I
was in touch with the fact that on those days I was not happy
when the class began. I was relieved and delighted when it
ended. . . . When I was with this group, I experienced feelings of loneliness, alienation, and isolation. I came to the
realization that when I entered the class I felt constricted. I
experienced a range of unpleasant feelings and chose not to
reveal them. I did not allow myself to smile and never
laughed during the class. I realized that I did not trust this
group to care about my presentation of course materials.

"I, who typically valued my way of being with others discovered, that it was my own behavior that was unacceptable. I resolved to change my behavior, to be more authentic in offering what I knew I could contribute to this seminar. This experience enabled me to move into the next phase of the discovery process.

"During this phase I became totally involved in the struggle to change. Self-dialogue and self-exploration were dominant methods of resolving the problem. To myself, I addressed the following questions and searched internally for answers:

1. What made my behavior during this seminar different from past behavior in similar situations?

2. How was my behavior serving me?

3. When I perceived "the group" as rejecting me, did I intend to include all members of the group?

4. Did I avoid contact with the students who were most critical of me?

5. What cues did I use to determine that I could not trust certain members of this group?

6. How did I go about alienating myself from some of the students?

7. How did I avoid assessing the students' behavior while making uncomfortable judgments about myself?

8. What did I do with the disturbing thoughts that were awakening in me during these class meetings?

9. What will prepare me to move on?

"The process involved assessing my strengths and considering the changes that would enable me to respond differently. What did I need in order to laugh again, to enjoy rich encounters and constructive confrontation with my students? What did I need to become alive again in my presentation of course materials and to enjoy myself as a teacher and my process of being me?

"As I considered these questions, I felt a heaviness lift from me and joy take over. Self-powers had been reawakened. I had come home to myself again, determined to create positive life with my students."

## FORGIVING ANOTHER

Emphasis on dialogue between self and other is at the heart of the heuristic investigation. In their study "The Psychology of Forgiving Another," Jan Rowe and colleagues (1989) comment on the effects of dialogue between the searcher and the phenomenon. Here is a brief excerpt from their study:

> [F]orgiveness is a process that begins when one person perceives oneself as harmed by another and ends in a psychological, if not face-to-face, reconciliation with the one who was perceived as hurtful. [p. 239]

> The resolution, in the form of forgiveness, appears to come to us in an unexpected context, often at an unexpected moment. And yet, as one is surprised by the resolution, it becomes apparent that, at some level, it was sought; one was willing to forgive and open to the possibility of resolution. It seems that this willingness is crucial for forgiveness to occur. . . . Experientially . . . the moment of forgiveness appears to be the moment of recognition that it has already occurred. Rather than being aware of changing, one realizes that one has changed, one has forgiven the other. [p. 241]

In seminars that I offered with teachers over 20 years, I recommended in class assignments that the teacher enter into an heuristic study of her or his experience of a disliked or rejected child. The teacher was asked to enter into at least one special encounter each day with the child and record it in a journal. Dramatic shifts occurred not only in the teacher's understanding of what it means to reject another person but also in understanding the relationship itself. Change occurred from rejection of the child to recognition, acceptance, and caring.

While encountering the phenomenon dialogically, the researcher is lifting out perceptions, feelings, and bodily expressions that lead to a change in the researcher's own attitude and behavior.

## THE HABIT OF SURVIVING

Kesho Yvonne Scott's (1991) study of the habit of surviving is a powerful example of the heuristic nature of self-searching and the uncovering of meaning. Habits of survival "refer to the external adjustments and internal adaptations that people make to economic exploitation and to racial and gender oppression. Such habits, first and foremost, are responses to pain and suffering that help lessen anger, give a sense of control and offer hope" (p. 10).

Here are some excerpts of Scott's depiction of the social-political context in which her own habits of surviving *were* generated:

> My story is a story of a black woman who survived by learning to be political—always at every moment, political. Born in the fifties and raised in the sixties, my physical, ideological, and social world was being reshaped by a spiraling number of interlocking social movements that changed society and expanded my hopes and possibilities far beyond my childhood dreams. . . . My story is about black womanhood in an era that offered more freedom to struggle against limited sex-roles, to put off or reject marriage and motherhood, and to benefit from the breakdown of racial barriers and conservative norms. I could travel, live alone, love, and date whomever I wanted, could work in traditionally male pro-

fessions, and could immerse myself in myriad cultural and politics lifestyles.

My story, then, my habit of surviving, centers around my unshakable belief that I was totally self-reliant and free of restraint. Knowing myself to be "po-li-ti-cal," I legitimized my beliefs and behaviors, no matter how silly, self-destructive, or hurtful they were, with the claim that I would never be trapped by the past because I knew how to manufacture my own freedom. My story is about being "liberated from" some things and about the painful trials and discovery of what I needed to be "liberated to." My habit of surviving was such that it never occurred to me that I might be arrogant before my time. [pp. 199–200]

## INTIMATE BONDING IN FRIENDSHIPS

Another example is borrowed from Kerry Moustakas's (1993) doctoral dissertation on intimate bonding in friendships.

Chem, a philosopher and educator, and I met on a bright, sunny early afternoon, in a completely private space, in his home. No other members of his family were present. Before we began the interview he handed me a written account of his thoughts on intimate bonding—as related to specific friendships. He shared his belief that intimate bonding in friendships contained both universal qualities and unique features that distinguished one friendship from another. The interview, he said, would focus on the unitary constituents of friendship. His written account concentrated on concrete, singular, incomparable friendships. Data both from his written statements and from the interview are included.

Once the interview began, the dialogue unfolded without interruption. So that the flow of his depiction will be continuous, I have not included my own comments (except in one instance), although they often generated important meanings and sparks of recognition and knowing between us. When I sensed that he was relaxed, I asked him to begin, to share with me his thoughts and feelings on the nature and substance of his experience of intimate bonding in friendships. He offers clear and incisive portrayals of what it means to enter into the process of creating intimate bonds in relationships.

"I have been very excited about this meeting and in the past several weeks, at various intervals, I have taken an opportunity to just stop and focus on the nature and meaning of intimate bonds in friendships. This brought into focus a number of people with whom I have created such bonds. I have paused and considered what this means; I have honored friendship by taking the time and the space to focus on it. . . . So many times, when I've been reading, suddenly a person would come into my vision. I would drift into what we share. All of this has happened since I first received your instructions which inspired me to concentrate on your topic.

"Something is there in each of my intimate friendships that calls out to me—a sudden and profound inner sense of knowing, of being drawn into a relationship by mysterious and tacit stirrings. That is true of all of my friendships—immediacy, openness and connectedness. They are always in process, always something of a freshness in my friendships, elements of exploring, searching, discovering, new meanings and new activities—the sense of being at home. There is never a need to explain, or to analyze or to question. Life just flows and continues and no matter how much time passes between our meetings, there is always a wholeness and a connectedness right from the start, and it is true with all of them . . . a sense, time and space that enriches the friendships.

"The intimate bonding of my friendships [has] undergone the test of time and [has] faced many ranges of feelings, and thoughts, and experiences, going all the way from the most joyous, exuberant, wondrous moments to some of the very painful, anguishing, despairing times, but none of these friends were only there in times of good fortune, and good things. They were always there in both extremes. The joy and happiness. And in the tragedies of illnesses and accidents. Each of us has always been present to the other.

"I have made some mistakes, some wrong choices in entering and creating intimate bonding in a friendship that did not succeed in overcoming the attractions of power, money, and status; friendships in which I had shared my most intimate thoughts, feelings, and aspirations as well as my work. I still don't know how to know the difference in those relationships that have been long term, intimate bonded friendships that have maintained a truth about their meaning and existence and that have endured and those that ended or have become limited. Perhaps there is always that risk. Perhaps there is something ultimately unpredictable about what will suddenly awaken in an intimate friendship that will alter the course of one's life and remain true and trusting throughout the relationship and those that have the essential *beginning*, caring, love, and acceptance but do not last. I have experienced this betrayal in three or four relationships and am now more cautious about intimate bondings in a new friendship."

As I immersed myself in the typed transcript and came to understand Chem's depiction of the experience of intimate bonding in friendships, certain themes stood out. I summarize these as follows:

1. Within intimate bonding are unifying and unitary qualities but there are also unique features, contents, and activities that distinguish one friendship from another.

2. Intimate friendships are characterized by sudden, immediate openings, freshness of dialogue and sharings, and connectedness and mutuality, in person-to-person interactions.

3. Within the intimate bonding of friendships, the persons explore ideas and meanings, search into their thoughts and feelings, discover new meanings, and create new activities.

4. The two persons are comfortable with each other, affirmed by each other, at home with each other and free to express themselves without monitoring their thoughts and feelings. "There is never a need to explain or to analyze or to question each other."

5. Freedom to be is a hallmark of intimate bonding in friendships—freedom to express oneself, in one's own tone of language, one's own words, without monitoring or censoring in any way, knowing that one will be accepted and valued in one's own self-expression.

6. In intimate bonding, the partners experience joy in being together. They know the wonder of adventure and surprise. They discover their own thoughts, feelings, meanings, who they are together, what they are moving toward in being and becoming.

7. In intimate friendships, the two persons express themselves as total human beings, including their sexual nature, but not through sexual intercourse which might narrow or focus the friendship on one segment of human encounter.

8. The partners in intimate bonding are there for one another in times of triumph and in times of tragedy and crisis.

9. Entering into an intimate friendship involves making a choice. The choice involves risk. The true relationship undergoes the test of time. It is long term, enduring, and withstands the challenges of geographical distance and time. In intimate bonding there is an unpredictability factor that may lead to betrayal and an end of the relationship.

10. There is no way of distinguishing the intimate, bonded friendships that endure the tests of time, space, and geographical distance and those that do not.

11. Intimate bonding in friendship is an unending process; it is never finished. It is continually unfolding in new directions, new sharings, new ways of fulfilling its potentials.

12. There is no imposition of role, title, or authority. Each person in the friendship has the power and authority of his or her own voice and the promise for being and growing in solitary and mutually rewarding ways.

## CONCLUDING COMMENTS

In reviewing the principles, values, and processes that are inherent in heuristic discovery, I am struck with the wonder of discovering that the only way one can truly know something is to go out to it, to return to it again and again, to immerse oneself in it completely in just what is there before one, and in one, looking, seeking, listening, hearing, touching, from many angles and perspectives, and vantage points, each time freshly so that there will be continual openings and learnings that will connect with each other, with prior perceptions and understandings, and with future possibilities. In other words, in heuristic focusing I immerse myself totally and completely in someone or something, take in everything that is offered, without bias or prejudgment. And then in my own conscious awareness, thought, and presence, I reflect on all that I have perceived and experienced—to know again and again the nature and meaning of phenomena, the ways of things and people, and the wonder of discoveries that not only open and extend perceptions of life but facilitate understandings and meanings within me. This connectedness between what is out there, in its appearance and reality, and what is within me in reflective thought and awareness, is in truth a wondrous gift of being human. But knowledge does not end with such moments of connectedness, understanding, and meaning. Such journeys open vistas of self and world, but they are also openings themselves to new journeys for uncovering knowledge—journeys within journeys, within journeys. This is perhaps the most telling reality of all, that each stopping place in heuristic discovery is but a pause. Satisfying as it is in itself, it is also the inspiration for new beginnings. There is no limit to our understanding or sense of fulfillment, no limit to knowledge of our own experience of any situation, thing, or person. We need only come to life again regarding some person, curiosity, problem, thing, puzzlement, and everything crystallizes in and through and beyond it. The whole process of being within something outside ourselves while being within ourselves, and relating these outer and inner connections and meanings, is infinite. This is the beauty of heuristic knowledge and discovery. It keeps us forever awake, alive, and renewed in our relationship to what is and what matters in life as well as what might be and will be.

# 3

# Discovery:
# Processes and Methods

In exploring an issue, problem, or question, I focus on what is immediately present in my conscious awareness, just as it is, on what stands out for me. I try to discover the meanings that live within me, that are before me in what I see, feel, think, and touch. Personal meanings are what matter. They provide the basis for my reflections and deliberations and ultimately for what is actual and real. My primary task is to accept, encourage, and support these meanings. I must let them be and in that letting be permit myself to create an essential clearing that makes discovery possible. Recognition of personal meanings opens the way to the development of comprehensive understanding and facilitates the making of authentic choices.

## THE PROCESSES OF DISCOVERY

In authentic discovery of knowledge, I do not look for hidden dynamics. I do not interpret reality or try to expose what is broken, distorted, or deviant in motivation or behavior. I receive what is present in my awareness, in the immediate appearance of things. I try not to get stuck on what is missing or not there in my life, on who I am not, or what I am not, on what I should be or might be. I set my gaze on just what is present in my consciousness, in the way of knowledge, understanding, meaning, and relationship.

In reflecting on my experience, I am aware of the value of beginning with my own perceptions, feelings, and intuitions of the way things are for me, internally and externally. I permit myself to let these subjective and objective meanings remain in my awareness, to wait in silence for the distinctive relationships to emerge, connections that mark my being, and offer something compelling and vital for understanding and action. This process cannot be hurried; it requires its own space and time. In the discovery process, I recognize the nature of my unfolding inner life. I receive the internal meaning as an invitation to pause, reflect on, and participate in the rhythms of self and world. I may recognize the conflicts, challenges, and discords as well as the flow, harmony, and balance that is in my life. The discovery process is a way to personal knowledge, personal power, and creative realization. It is a resource for strengthening individuality and for recognizing the validity of one's choices, permitting what is in truth to be recognized and confirmed.

In this process, for example, I may be filled with delight, entranced by visions of knowing, images of being, and feelings that connect me to myself and others. I embrace delight in my life, take it fully into my being. I am moved to express its meanings, perhaps through descriptive writing or in conversations with myself and others, or in the creation of poems and stories. In the process of discovering the meaning of delight, I grant delight full recognition and expression. For a while nothing else exists. Delight becomes my opening to the world, an awakening of unique and joyous possibilities in my life. In this way delight forms its ways and bursts forth in its own directions, bringing with it the "shimmering essence that lies within appearances" (McGlashan 1976, p. 156).

In delight, the world takes on a richness, a kind of playfulness and childlikeness that frees me to move effortlessly, with the lightness of being. I envision possibilities for fresh experience, for encountering others, for appreciating the wonders of love and nature. Expressions of delight are in every breath I take. Like a dance, delight becomes the center of a life that brings me into touch with people who are honest, true, affirming. It facilitates a sense of belonging and the development of a sense of self and community. Delight is a way of being, and a way to harmony and laughter. In delight I find a receptiveness and readiness to see things differently, to know what is present in its actual presence, and to embrace what is alive and joyous in my life. My energy feels timeless and inexhaustible. The discovery process enables me to recognize and know what delight is and brings me into touch with delight's possibilities.

In considering the discovery process, I have observed three phases: first, an *initial breakthrough*, the *revealment* of something new, an *opening receptiveness* that inspires me to look again in a fresh way. Next, I become aware of *recovering* something lost, bringing into consciousness something that has been dominant, missing or is unfinished. This involves a return to prior experience, a bearing with something that previously seemed unbearable, suffering with it, struggling with it, allowing myself to perceive it openly and accept its existence. It is as if, at last, there is a recognition, a calling from life itself that gives birth to something previously unspoken or abandoned, and denied, but that is now allowed to be. The recovering phase enables me to live with the rejection, to face the fear, to listen to voices of the past, my own and others, with new and different ears, until what has been hurt or tampered with rises once more, as an expression of my own being. In the process, I recover something of myself and am in touch with resources that enable me to view the situation differently and to see my own possibilities for moving beyond the fear, pain, and apparent hopelessness.

In confronting an issue or problem, the final step involves a *discovery phase* in which there is a *realization* of a new meaning or new direction, the emergence of an insight or understanding, the development of a project, the forming of new understanding and relationship. In this phase, I look ahead to what can be and will be, to what I am attuned to in a positive sense, to realities of the present and possibilities of the future. I have enhanced my sense of self and strengthened my self-confidence and personal power. What was unexpressed and undeveloped can now be explored in seeking an effective resolution and action.

To summarize: In the discovery process, first, there is the revealment of something new in awareness and the determination to let that linger and be. Next, the discovery takes the person back to earlier times, people, and events, when something of personal value and potential had been thwarted and interfered with or lost. What had been dominant, denied, and abandoned is now recovered and approached with new eyes, with an openness and receptiveness to what is genuinely one's own. This leads to an acceptance, understanding, and realization of new directions for one's life.

The process of awakening to what is, recovering what has been lost, and discovering new possibilities for living is depicted in Rilke's (1941) poem "Now the Hour Bows Down":

*Discovery* of what is:

> Now the hour bows down, it touches me, throbs
> metallic and lucid and bold:
> my senses are trembling. I feel my own power—
> on the plastic day I lay hold.

*Recovery* of perceptual acuity:

> Until I perceived it, no thing was complete,
> but waited, hushed, unfulfilled.

> My vision is ripe, to each glance like a bride
> comes softly the thing that was killed.

*Discovery* of realities and possibilities:

> There is nothing too small, but my tenderness paints
> it large on a background of gold,
> and I prize it, not knowing whose soul at the sight,
> released, may unfold . . . [p. 11]

## SHIFT IN LANGUAGE

In phenomenal discovery, the individual abandons what *is not*. Literally, there is a radical shift of language, from words of striving toward making up for what is not, of wanting and hoping for what has not been and cannot be, of trying to change what is into something not changeable—one's way of being, a relationship, another person, a feeling, situation, or event. A shift in language when one looks at the phenomenon just as it appears, with an attitude of letting it be, searching to understand just what exists in one's immediate awareness. This may involve concentrating for a while on what has been missing or what is unfinished, but the concentration and receptiveness in the discovery process moves the person to a different language, words that embrace the genuine and eliminate the nonexistent and the counterfeit. The discovery process requires that one welcome just what is in one's awareness and what can become in an authentic sense. In phenomenal discovery, there is a shift from the language of nonbeing and nonpresence to the language of being and presence. This ends the self-destructive denials and enables the person to leap forth to the language of hope, determination, possibility. A new sense of self emerges with new words, new meanings, and new directions. The processes of phenomenal discovery lead inevitably to enhanced self-efficacy, in use of one's own resources in perceptions, analyses, and decision making. There is within one renewed self-

awareness, a willfulness and determination to find a path
to creative life and to pursue it. This excerpt from Hesse's
*Siddhartha* (1951) beautifully describes the process:

> Siddhartha reflected deeply as he went on his way. He real-
> ized that he was no longer a youth; he was now a man. He
> realized that something had left him, like the old skin that a
> snake sheds. Something was no longer in him, something that
> had accompanied him right through his youth and was part
> of him . . . I was afraid of myself, I was fleeing from myself.
> I was seeking Brahman, Atman, I wished to destroy myself
> to get away from myself, in order to find the unknown inner-
> most, the nucleus of all things, Atman, Life, the Divine, the
> Absolute. But by doing so, I lost myself on the way . . . Sid-
> dhartha stood still and for a moment an icy chill stole over
> him. He shivered inwardly like a small animal, like a bird
> or a hare, when he realized how alone he was. . . . At that
> moment, when the world around him melted away, when he
> stood alone like a star in the heavens, he was overwhelmed
> by a feeling of icy despair, but he was more firmly himself
> than ever. That was the last shudder of his awakening, the
> pains of birth. [p. 37]

## PHENOMENOLOGICAL METHODS

During the discovery process, I have employed methods
borrowed from phenomenology but based on my own in-
terpretive meanings (Moustakas 1994a). These are *Epochē, Reflective Description,* and *Imaginative Variation.* In Epochē, I set
aside my own preconceptions of what things mean. I enter
into an openness, recognition, and response to what is immediately before me. I am inspired to view whatever stands out,
in this other person's frame of reference, as the most valid
entrance into this other person's world. In therapy, for example, I wait with patience, until the person is able to set
aside the anger, rage, or despair over past cruelties, the damage of guilt, the animosities, resentments, and anxieties. I

look for an opening, a beginning, a fresh start, a new language, where I can jump into something solid, something that I can take hold of and connect with in the immediate life of the person. Whatever emerges offers something that can be explored and actualized.

The process of Epochē paves the way for Reflective Description. In this process, I elaborate and explicate what is actually present. Using this method with myself, I return to sources of energy and life to retrieve what has been lost, missing, or broken. I surrender to whatever is present, carry it into my world. In life with others, I search for mutual rhythms, glimmerings of who and what we are, possibilities for life. From this perspective, we are able to recover sources of being that have been interfered with, that have blocked and restrained us. We struggle with the discovery process and resolve to let the miracle that is within us live again, as in Kazantzakis's (1975) *Report to Greco*:

As I turn over the yellowed pages of my journal, it becomes clear that nothing died. Everything was simply asleep inside me. Look how all has awakened now, how everything rises from the worn, half-indecipherable pages to become monasteries, monks, paintings, and the sea once more! . . . When, completing our circle, we finally returned to Daphne on Christmas Eve in order to depart, the most unexpected, most decisive miracle was awaiting us. Though it was the heart of winter, there in a small, humble orchard was an almond tree in bloom!

Seizing my friend's arm, I pointed to the blossoming tree. "Angelos," I said, "during the whole of this pilgrimage our hearts have been tormented by many intricate questions. Now, behold the answer!"

My friend riveted his blue eyes upon the flowering almond tree and crossed himself, as though doing obeisance before a holy wonder-working icon. He remained speechless for a long moment. Then, speaking slowly, he said, "A poem is rising to my lips, a tiny little poem: a haiku."

He looked again at the almond tree.

*I said to the almond tree,*
*"Sister, speak to me of God,"*
*And the almond tree blossomed.* [pp. 222–223]

Throughout the discovery process, the key is description of what is, the issue, problem, concern, question; description of thoughts, feelings, time and space, relationship to self and others; description of people, rooms, places, things, faces, body expressions, textures (heavy-light, rough-smooth, hot-cold, foggy-clear, tight-open). The following is an example of a recent traumatic experience of my own in which description enabled me to find the light in the darkness. Permitting the experience to remain in my consciousness, I was able to recover resources for coping with it and for moving on to other activities and challenges.

"My world these past weeks lives harshly inside me. It closes in on me. I am aware of its gripping tentacles, its sharp edges grabbing me, at unexpected hours, from all sides, frightening and subduing me, narrowing the range of my experience, and restraining my words and breathing. What is happening anyway, in this overwhelmingly restricted space, in this lingering sadness? How one-dimensional my life has been lately, rooted in *their* directions, in institutional credentials, absorbed by accreditation policies and agencies. In the process I have pushed my own self out of the way, my exploring, inventive, free self, my freedom to wonder and simply to be. I am lost in a paper world, of reports, and policies, and external 'self-studies,' obsessed with other people's deadlines, with forms and files, and schedules, with staple machines, copy machines, spindles, and computers, with finances and long-range plans, with all the things that *they* say are essential to achievement and progress.

"All at once I am feeling the anguish of what is missing and lost. I want my old world back. I want to enter into my solitude and meditative life, my independent studies, new learnings, and spontaneous adventures. I want my silence back, my private thoughts, my quiet world of reveries and wanderings, my peculiar and idiosyncratic ways, my hours of writing and thinking and simply being. I want to be free to wander, and get lost, and be timeless. I want once more to be able to take my thoughts all the way to fulfillment, and, more than anything, I just want once again to be an individual and to be a creative person, not just in the middle-of-the-night but everyday, day in, day out, the way it used to be. I want my life back.

"As I write, I feel the painfulness of this loss of being. I am aware of how this surrendering of myself has happened in the past and how terribly alone I have felt lately, alone in a world of people, progress, achievement, money, alone in the feeling that there is really no one who understands what such self-surrendering means, that progress and achievement of justice in social and political matters does not reduce the sense of self-isolation and loneliness, or the hunger for quiet, anonymous living, for creative solitude and being. I know clearly in this moment what has been set aside and abandoned, the passional dimensions of myself, essential sides of being. No matter how important credentials are, they will never satisfy the hungering spirit, the being alive as a solitary self, the yearning to pursue my own questions, to discover my own meanings, to explore unfinished urgings for learning and knowing and active personal living. Who would understand this inward sense of emptiness that haunts me, in a life filled with urgency and crises, a life that moves too fast, demands that cover the hours of day and night, where things must be finished in a hurry, and where there is always a next thing and a next and a next thing in an endless series of projects, tasks, requirements.

"Sometimes I feel myself slipping away. But, I must not show the crumbling, or the inward weeping that would reduce my energy and outward purpose. Within is the desire to return to isolation and loneliness, but I must remain competent and productive, all the while knowing that what I really want from time to time is the joy and serenity of being nobody, of being lost, unafraid, unchallenged, of not being, of nothing.

"Strange, that after all these months, I am just now coming to a realization of my loss of solitude, just now taking an inward turn and seeing the way things are. I am in this moment fully present, to this very solitude, to this self-reflection, aware that my life must change, that it will change, that I will find a way to restore my privacy, my independent studies, my joy in meditation, my awakening and fulfillment in writing. Within me is a growing resolution to return to my self, to be immersed once more in creative wanderings, to take time to be with nature, to collaborate with its resources and offerings, to be with myself and others again in timeless ways. A light is breaking through these institutional shadows, a definite movement toward self-space and self-time, a sureness that there will be a return, a deepening of breath, a stretching of body, a nourishment of soul. Something is lifting, there is an old-new world ahead, a turning that is genuinely mine, visions and thoughts that will bring unity and fulfillment to my life, that will restore me to my own silence and solitude, and that will enable self-creations to flow."

From descriptions, like these of my own awakening to the imperative of silence and solitude, a clear account of the issue, problem, relationship, or concern is explicated. The description is brought to a place of fullness and clarity. The description reveals what is, its nature, state, direction, and meaning.

The descriptive process draws everything in, lets everything in, lets it be. In the process of this letting be of what is in the person's world, certain universal themes often stand out—for example, love, power, autonomy, loneliness, self-esteem. Each is considered in its possible meanings. Through Imaginative Variation, alternatives are examined, possibilities are tested, and many different meanings are envisioned and explicated.

In the imaginative varying of possibilities for new life, there is a sense, a perspective, based on knowledge and experience, an incorporation of the freshness of what is newly born, the creative awakening of the discovery process. In Imaginative Variation, each position, in its presence, and from the extreme, is considered. Intuition, hunches, movements, from the known to mystery, and to knowing anew. Each is tapped as a way to insight and action. In Imaginative Variation, one must be willing to permit alternatives to enter consciousness, to consider various pathways for living, and to direct one's life into fruitful channels of experience.

The shift from loss to gain, from *blindness* to inner vision, from detachment to involvement, from absence to presence, is beautifully described and explicated by Lusseyran (1987) in the following passages:

> All I needed was to leave my hands to their own devices. I had nothing to teach them, and besides, since they began working independently, they seemed to foresee everything. Unlike eyes, they were in earnest, and from whatever direction they approached an object they covered it, tested its resistance, leaned against the mass of it and recorded every irregularity in its surface. They measured it for height and thickness, taking in as many dimensions as possible. But most of all, having learned that they had fingers, they used them in an entirely new way.
>
> When I had eyes, my fingers used to be stiff, half dead at the ends of my hands, good only for picking up things. But now each one of them started out on its own. They explored things separately, changed levels and, independently of each other, made themselves heavy or light. . . .
>
> Touching the tomatoes in the garden, and really touching them, touching the walls of the house, the materials of the curtains or a clod of earth is surely seeing them as fully as eyes can see. But it is more than seeing them, it is tuning in on them and allowing the current they hold to connect with

one's own, like electricity. To put it differently, this means
an end of living in front of things and a beginning of living
with them. [pp. 26–28]

In dealing with a problem like rejection, after first considering its personal meanings from one's own experiences,
through imaginatively varying the perspectives, a totally
different meaning emerges. Its nature is more fully developed as one examines the meanings and essences of rejection in one's own life and then how others experience rejection; how they might view a rejecting event, situation, or
person; how rejection is expressed by one's mother, father,
daughter, son, or one's friend, minister, or teacher.

Imaginative Variation is a way to live out and own a full
development of the meanings of an experience. In the process, ever-recurring awarenesses emerge. We describe them
as they arise in our consciousness.

Salk (1983) presents a process of imaginative discovery in
his book *Anatomy of Reality*:

In order to understand what follows it will be necessary for
me to refer to certain effects of inverted perspective which I
have found valuable in my scientific work and which I have
also used as a device to understand the human condition.
I do not remember exactly at what point I began to apply this
way of examining my experience, but very early in my life I
would imagine myself in the position of the object in which
I was interested. Later, when I became a scientist, I would
picture myself as a virus, or as a cancer cell, for example, and
try to sense what it would be like to be either. I would also
imagine myself as the immune system, and I would try to
reconstruct what I would do as an immune system engaged
in combating a virus or cancer cell.

When I had played through a series of such scenarios on a
particular problem and had acquired new insights, I would
design laboratory experiments accordingly. I soon found
myself in a dialogue with nature using viruses, immune sys-

tems, and other phenomena to ask questions in the form of experiments and then waiting for an answer. Based upon the results of the experiment, I would then know what questions to ask next, until I learned what I wanted to know, or until I went as far as I could go. [p. 7]

Salk's discovery process includes the following:

1. *Growing quiet and listening,* stopping the noises of thinking, creating an inner stillness and readiness, being alert to inner dialogue

2. *Awareness of a translucent quality in all things,* the presence of a dancing concentration and deepening of all that is, the ability to invert perspectives

3. *Playfulness,* exploratory engagement, body awarenesses and experiences of shifting realities

4. *The being of self and other,* entering fully, imagining shifting presences and meanings

5. E*stablishing relationships to the unknown,* the unfolding nature of mystery, the sense of timelessness and limitless space, and the relationship of self to other, the ability to change frames of reference and invert realities

## ACTIVITY TO GUIDE DISCOVERY PROCESS

From the principles underlying the Discovery-Recovery-Discovery process, I outline the following activity as a guide to the unraveling of an issue, problem, or question.

1. Move off alone. Find a quiet place where you might achieve a feeling of relaxation and inward peace.

2. Select an issue in your own development or identity, or in a significant relationship, one that is of continuing con-

cern perhaps with reference to freedom, honesty, love, autonomy, loneliness, power, self-esteem, or some other value that challenges, puzzles, worries, or disturbs you.

3. As much as possible, set aside all biases, beliefs, and understandings regarding the issue or problem. Engage in Epochē in order to discover something fresh and new regarding the issue or relationship. Let yourself reveal what emerges in this pure and open presence.

4. Describe your perceptions, feelings, thoughts, body awarenesses; the textures, nuances, and flavors of the issue or relationship; and the awakening that has emerged from your reflective description. Include everything that has contributed to the meaning and development of the issue or problem.

5. Read your description. Underline each key word or phrase that points to what is particularly essential and relevant to the issue, problem, or relationship.

6. Cluster the words or phrases into key themes. Briefly explicate each theme to include many possible meanings or alternate views.

7. From the understanding that you derive, what course of action might you pursue to resolve the issue or problem? What has awakened in you that would lead you to being effective as a self in changing the situation? How might you approach the situation of relationship? Depict the resolution in some creative form, a poem, story, or drawing; an anecdote, parable, or metaphor.

## CONCLUDING COMMENTS

In closing this discussion of the discovery process, I want to emphasize that however far removed we may be from our own life, no matter how often we may depart or stray from

ourselves, forever and always there will be a space and resources within to recover what has been lost or missing and
to discover new ways of being and action. Through the discovery process, our dreams will rise once more; we will realize more completely the truth of our own existence and arrive
at an understanding that will move us toward the light of
our own being and a genuine and creative life with others.
However limited life with others may be, the way out is
always within; a personal solitude and inquiry awaits that
is the only true path to our unfolding destiny.

# 4

**Conventional versus
Meditative Thinking**

In a basic sense, individuals in contemporary society have lost touch with how to think reflectively and qualitatively. Communication is often inauthentic and manipulative. Daily I witness the failure of people to pause and allow silent moments to open space that invites thoughtfulness. I have also observed the failure to recognize the significance of gradualness and patience in communication of ideas and feelings. We have forgotten that "[i]n thinking all things become solitary and slow" and that "patience nurtures magnanimity" (Heidegger 1971, p. 9).

Heidegger (1971), in his writings, set out to focus on the problem of thinking, its nature and challenge. He emphasized that "the thing before our eyes," the essentials of authentic being, human presence and openness, are gifts of genuine thinking.

In thinking, we return to meanings that recognize rhythm and timing, that facilitate the deepening and extending of thought.

Thinking is a process of gathering words and holding them before us, focusing on what is in us, taking to heart what captivates us, what stands out as thought or question, so that we may discover the nature and truth of what is and what is not.

Thinking itself is a human *gift*, an act of human construction. What we love is thought-provoking, alive within us, and as Holderin exclaims, the deepest of thought "loves what is most alive" (Heidegger 1971, p. 20).

What is called thinking can be approached from an examination of what it is that commands us to think, the prerequisites of thinking. Thinking calls to us, requires our attention, invites our concentration. Thinking "brings our essential nature into the keeping of thought. . . , demands for itself that it be tended, cared for, husbanded in its own essential nature, by thought" (Heidegger 1968, p. 121).

In thinking authentically we are called by what is in us, by what we are most strongly attracted to, by what needs to be thought.

We are challenged to regard thinking with care, the guardian of our destiny as human beings. When one is called upon to think, one is called by what is most thought-provoking, by "opinions, ideas, reflections, propositions, notions that provoke, challenge, and evoke compelling thoughts" (Heidegger 1968, p. 144).

Thinking is something to be thankful for, the gathering of all that concerns us, all that we care for, what touches us as human beings. By giving thought its freedom, we understand the uniqueness of human expression.

Thought recalls what it is connected to, what it must be concentrated in; what it must dwell on, in memory; what is and what can be. Something holds us in thought; we focus and concentrate on it. That something often moves us to the past to which it is grounded and from which we gather images and symbols, moments of awareness and understanding, ideas and assumptions, beliefs and judgments. In thought and care, we move with patience and gradualness to the immediate moment and view it in its distinctive presence. We open ourselves to an expanding awareness and knowledge, a more complete understanding, a deeper level of meaning. The process of discovering meaning in thought is in the nature of thought. Genuine thinking alters our ideas, understandings, assumptions, and judgments.

The basic character of thinking is constituted by propositions and, ordinarily (Heidegger 1968, pp. 154–157), involves calculating and problem solving. Yet such conventional thinking fails to recognize the opening of Being, what is present in reality. A representational form of thinking gives reasons but departs from what is present in its presence (Heidegger 1972, p. 56).

Heidegger states that the decisive requirement for thinking is that each person respond to the way of thinking as a process. Thus, what is essential to thinking cannot be satisfied solely by assumptions, propositions, and factual evidence. The very process of discovering what is essential in thinking invites a process of collaboration of oneself with what is, a unity of subject and object, of thought and action. Such a process is not the way of quantitative thinkers. Heidegger (1968) asserts that "today, when we know much too much and form opinions much too quickly, when we compute and pigeonhole everything in a *flash*—today there is not room at all left for the hope that presentation of a matter might in itself be powerful enough to set in motion any fellow thinking, which, prompted by the showing of the matter, would join us in our way" (p. 171).

Calculative thinking is representational of what is typical of objects and things. It is lineal, goal directed, a moving toward, "for" something, and "in order to." Meditative thinking is nonlineal. It is a response to what is, an awareness of horizons, thinking that is both open and bounded to what is given. Meditative thinking opens up a new ground of meaning, a releasement toward things, an openness to mystery that leads to new understanding of Being, to creation of what is, to what is given. It enables the fulfillment of a crucial dimension of nature. The poetic is a kind of thinking that calculated thought fails to reach (Heidegger 1977, p. 343).

Calculative thinking is characterized by methods of approaching things, dealing with and manipulating them.

In meditative thinking, the person opens to Being, to self-disclosure, and dwells in whatever awakens in one's consciousness. Meditative thinking involves an awareness of the field, a field that has no fixed limits (Heidegger 1966, p. 29), a way of building and enabling things to come to light (Heidegger 1977, pp. 321–323).

Meditative thinking lies before us and takes to heart what is. That which calls to us is blossoming, gleaming, resting, and aching in thought. What calls us is a presence: "To be present is to come close by, to be here in contrast and conflict with to be away" (Heidegger 1968, p. 236).

The presence of what is present arises from unconcealment, demands unconcealment. Thinking that is open discloses itself and abides in thought. The qualities of creative presence in thinking are "the rising from concealedness, the entry into unconcealedness, the coming and going away, the duration, the gathering, the radiance, the rest, the hidden suddenness of possible absenting" (Heidegger 1968, p. 237). These values are lost when thinking is fixed on objectivity, on conceiving, grasping, and manipulating thought.

The essential nature of thinking is determined "by what there is to be thought about: the presence of what is present, the Being of beings"(Heidegger 1968, p. 144).

The phenomenological approach to thinking has emphasized "the things themselves." This necessarily requires that the thing show itself. For something to show itself there must be an opening. This in turn rests upon thought being free to illuminate what is there (Heidegger 1972, p. 64). Openness grants to meditative thinking the passage through which it thinks (Heidegger 1972, pp. 64–65). Heidegger (1972) emphasizes that we "[l]ook for nothing behind phenomena: they themselves are what is to be learned" (pp. 65–66). In meditative thinking, we allow *what is* to be; we permit the phenomena to teach us, let them say something to us that will illuminate our thoughts in their essences. Thinking that follows the call "to the thing itself" is already admitted to opening. Heidegger (1972) elaborates, "The opening grants first of all the possibility of a path to presence and grants the possible presencing of that presence itself. . . . The quiet heart of the opening is the place of stillness from which alone the possibility of the belonging together of Being and thinking, that is, the presence and perceiving that can arise at all" (p. 68).

What is present in Being lets something appear and show opening; opening something means to make light, to illuminate. "The phenomenon itself, the opening, sets up the task of learning from it while questioning it, that is of letting it say something to us. The opening gathers and protects everything. Something can radiate only if openness has already been granted" (Heidegger 1972, p. 285). Thus, the task of thinking is to be open to whatever is present in consciousness, to let it be present to say something to us, without filtering it, censoring it or changing it in any way.

To think genuinely means to accept whatever is as it is. "To embrace a 'thing' or a 'person' in its essence means to love it, to favor it. It is on the strength of enabling by favoring that something is properly able to be. Favoring Being enables thinking" (Heidegger 1977, p. 196). Openness and presence, "favoring of Being," facilitate the unfolding of thinking in its most fundamental and authentic way.

Meditative thinking invites food for thought, a fresh perspective, a new set of ideas and values, a regard for thinking, a way to bringing one's being into the open and thus offering an authentic presence for discovering *what is*, what advances thinking, what offers an invitation to others to contribute to a deepening of understanding and knowledge. In meditative thinking, thought and thinker are united in the process of thinking. The unity creates an open field, inviting creation of a journey that extends human meaning and experience, offering a lighting and a clearing of what is, letting thinking be, thus deepening and extending understanding, meaning, and truth.

**5**

---

# The Meaning
# of Relationship

Every relationship contains within it seeds for emergence and growth as well as seeds of decay, stagnation, and death. Early in the development of a significant relationship, patterns are established that influence not only its nature but the nature and quality of other future relationships. With focus and effort, it is possible to transcend these early patterns, to understand them and set them aside, to begin freshly in entering a new relationship. It is possible to approach life with a readiness to create new patterns and ways of being with others.

In this chapter, I shall examine the meaning of relationship; rhythms and rituals; and the concepts of receptivity, attunement, and bodying forth as basic conditions for positive, intimate life with others. I shall also discuss Being-In, Being-For, and Being-With as processes that move relationships toward fullness, creativity, and significance.

## ROOTS OF RELATIONSHIP

The term *relate* is paradoxical. It comes from the Latin word *refero*. *Suffer* is derived from a similar Latin root, *suffero*. Thus, they share a common base, *fero*, "to bear," "to carry," "to put up with." In every genuine relationship, to achieve ultimate meaning, we must submit to it, undergo it, endure it, suffer with it (Lockhart 1978). We must return again and again to its nature and its unfolding patterns, carry something of it with us. We must grapple with the intimacies of relationship, must surrender to its ups and downs, and live with its burdens and stresses.

Repetition is an essential aspect of relationship. We return to the same scenes, the same situations, the same people; we make the same mistakes. Lockhart (1978) has emphasized that the qualities of repetition and return are necessary in going through the distortions, agonies, and pain of relationships. He states that we are brought *back* to the same place in relationships because we have never really left, that something still remains in thinking and feeling for us to go *through* —thus the ever-recurrent cycle of misery, denial, and failure; boredom, emptiness, and despair.

In the authentic relationship, there is a facing up to the feelings and issues, an exercise of wills, without the will on either side being negated, impaired, or broken. The will ignites the fires of determination and enables one to face the old patterns of criticism, adversity, and rejection; enables one to live with the negative feelings and thoughts while creating new images and meanings in the process.

Perhaps not all the suffering embedded in going through relationship completely ends. No matter how many times one returns, one discovers new perspectives and new meanings, no matter how many new and positive relationships have been formed. Perhaps there will always be something of the pain, violence, or loss that will remain as a reminder of the roots of our journeys with others, as a marking that alerts us when we move toward dangerous and destructive passages, as history and recollection influence our future choices and commitments.

What assists us in overcoming the harmful roots of relationship is a new relationship, the presence of a sensitive and caring human being, a friend, teacher, counselor, or therapist. The new relationship is anchored in the reality of one person's presence to another, in the being there, and in the safety, security, compassion, and acceptance of this other person.

In a dialogue with Carl Rogers, Paul Tillich called this affirmation and acceptance of one person by another *a listening love*. Tillich, quoted in *Carl Rogers: Dialogues* (Rogers 1989), describes listening love as a love that follows no abstract values but is concrete to the situation "and out of its listening to this very moment gains its decision for action and its inner feeling of satisfaction" (p. 78).

The will is indispensable in every genuine relationship. The challenge is to see it through, to direct it in terms of what it is, to keep it alive and moving in positive ways. The will is the necessary source of power for the required "againness" of relationship, for the "bearing with" its vicissitudes, its shifts and turns, and its crises. Expressions of will may lead to obstinance, stubbornness, and perversity, but such expressions also create hope that moves fear to acts of courage, impotency to a sense of power, and desire to actualization. Without the will the person is not present; the will is the individual voice, the gestures and words of an authentic being.

Going through a relationship means facing polarities within one's self. It means challenging the desire to hold onto fixed patterns rather than let go; the desire to repeat rather than to risk new experience; to remain passive rather than be assertive; to live in the past rather than in the present. It means facing the fear of trying again, undergoing the dangers, facing the old suffering; the fear of going around and around, awakening the old tortures of darkness. In essence, it means coming face to face with the heaviness of being and the uncertainties and dangers of entering into a new relationship, exploring extremes, swinging freely between the polarities of trust and distrust, openness and guardedness, spontaneity and caution, and ultimately emerging with a way of being that ends the neurotic quest and terminates the chronic denial and self-abnegation. The new relationship must be anchored in the reality of one person's presence to another; in the safety, security, compassion, and acceptance of this other person. Such a relationship challenges us to find our rhythms and to create rituals that will sustain its distinctiveness, uniqueness, and character.

## RHYTHMS AND RITUALS

Many years ago I discovered the significance of rhythms and rituals in my encounters with very young infants. After prolonged efforts of parents and others to still a screaming, flailing, inconsolable baby, when I held the infant and moved in synchronicity with the infant, I learned to locate within myself complementary rhythms, bodily positions that would be congruent with the infant's needs. When I was successful, a peacefulness would occur. To reach this place, the infant and I would undergo a remarkable series of gyrations, shifts, and imbalances. In the process of experimentation, invention, and creative alteration of bodily postures, we would discover a harmonious inward place, distinct and clear to both of us. We would rock peacefully together, becoming relaxed and comfortable, mutually connected. In a relatively short period, perhaps after four or five such encounters, the infant and I would have developed a very special and trusting relationship. Our entire communication was based in feeling rhythms, interactions that created intimate expressions, growing ties.

Since discovering the power of positive rhythms, I have found ways of relating significantly with the indifferent or frozen adult, the angry child, the frightened youth, the restless infant. No explaining, analyzing, reflecting, words, or silences are able to connect with a person who is intensely distressed and unhappy.

In Weems's (1975) study of rhythms in the African-American personality, he emphasizes:

> Rhythm is the pulse of the unitary vitalism which flows through and permeates the African's mind and world. It is manifested in everything from black movements to black speech, and, in more or less subtle forms, in all aspects of black life. It is simultaneously the essence of the oneness of the African wherever he is and the motivation for unification which characterizes the proverbial search of the African spirit. When disorder occurs—be it manifested physically, mentally, or spiritually—the disruption emanates from a disturbance in the rhythm which is the African's gauge of oneness. Order is restored when he attains a reestablishment of social equilibrium with his brothers and sisters. [p. 67]

From his own autobiographic experiences as a farmer, Roads (1987) offers an example of rhythmic attunement to natural phenomena. An encounter with his wife illustrates attunement to the rhythms of nature.

> One evening, while sitting relaxed in our living room, she glanced at me. "The cows want moving," she suddenly announced.
>
> I snorted with indignation. Her statement seemed a challenge and I responded.
>
> "Right! Just to prove you're wrong, we'll drive up there tomorrow at nine o'clock, and you can see for yourself all the contented cows on plenty of pasture."
>
> In my smug satisfaction, I burrowed back into my book.
>
> Next morning at nine o'clock, Treenie and I drove up to the back paddock. Shock! Practically the entire herd of cows was standing impatiently at the gate, waiting to be let out. I gaped at them, not willing to meet Treenie's eyes. You can imagine her next comment!

In two investigations of rhythmic interaction in which I served as research guide, the impact of rhythm on the development of relationships was studied and elucidated. Jayne Cohen (1981) studied rhythm in her efforts to establish relationships with autistic children. She collected 140 descriptions of rhythmic interactions. These involved moments of mirroring, physical contacts, and unusual forms of verbal and non-verbal communications. Her rhythmic connections with the autistic child facilitated a shift from isolation to an I-Thou relationship. Here is one example.

> I sit across from the child, observing for some time. . . . I immerse myself in the child's motions, rhythms, and idiosyncratic movements, so that the movements begin to feel a part of me. When I am satisfied the movements feel familiar, I slowly begin to mimic what the child in front of me is doing. This involves copying the child's body movements, noises, breathing patterns, and rhythms as exactly and as intensely as I am able. . . .
>
> I watch for clues that tell me, for example, if I may move closer, or if I may expand the motion and begin to touch a child.
>
> Sometimes, I may try to reach out quickly and gently touch the child in a playful manner. Then depending on what response I receive, I move on from there, following what my intuition, sensitivity, and skill tell me to do. In other instances, I may add my own variation to the existing rhythms . . . so that, in essence, my movements jar the child's, in a playful, loving way, and bring us into direct physical contact. . . .
>
> Shawn and I make contact through a game of football. Our game begins without any words, just the passing of a toy football back and forth. For the moment, we are basking in the pleasure of each other's company. We throw the football high into the air, over our heads, making our bodies stretch as we reach to catch it before it bounces. We fling the ball to one another, passing it to the left, then to the right, upwards, then downwards. We throw the ball one-handed, under our legs, between our legs, then back to back with eyes shut tight.

Shawn initiates and I follow; each of us brings to the game
our own inventive ways. [pp. 114–115]

In Shaw's (1989) investigation of interaction rhythms, he
derived the following core themes of effective synchronicity:

1. *Openness and Expansiveness*
   It's like giving one heart space; connection between mind
   and heart . . . like a channel that's open. . . . It's . . . back of
   you, in front of you, and on the sides of you, beneath you.
   . . . [Synchronistic rhythm in a relatlonship]: is like a fire on a
   winter's night.

2. *Loosening Boundaries of the Self*
   The boundaries of my body spread, dissipate. . . . There is
   no resistance. . . . I lose myself in it. . . . Being with someone
   where it feels safe and very comfortable and very easy and
   with a sense of . . . boundaries . . . dropping off.

3. *Positive Energy*
   The air between us is filled with energy, positive energy.
   It's a very mystical thing. . . . It's exciting. It's uplifting. It gives
   me the extra adrenaline rush to keep going.

4. *Focus and Absorption*
   There is nothing else around us. . . . The whole world is
   blocked out. . . . It is just us . . . carried away with the exchange
   (between us) and lost in the sense of being totally absorbed
   (with each other).

5. *Movement beyond the Ordinary*
   My senses were heightened. I saw nature and colors more
   vividly; a heightened state of consciousness. . . . My physical
   limits are not as important. . . . Moving forward into something new . . . gets my process moving faster, stronger, and
   deeper (p. 50).

Without rhythmic attunement, intimate connections with
others is not possible; meanings are limited and development
of relationships is thwarted. Positive rhythm encourages,

invites, and inspires openness and growth, self-disclosure, experimentation and risk.

Another process that offers significant pathways to connection with others is entered via the rituals that we employ. In every significant meeting, rituals create bonds and connect persons with a unique reality. Rituals create desires, hopes, and new intentions. As a child I began each day with an early awakening that involved specific movements, meditations, rubbing of eyes, shakings, turnings of my body, listening to sounds outside the window, and watching the movements of early morning clouds. These rituals gave the morning a special and unique meaning. They often enabled me to focus on a single event that was to be the source of particular challenge or excitement. Rituals belong only to the persons who create them. They are distinctive pathways through which individuals create ties. They guard a relationship and keep it from being invaded by others' expectations or needs.

The dwindling of rituals is a sign that a relationship is stagnating and growing cold. Rituals initiate the bonding process. A fine example of this process is presented in Saint-Exupery's (1943) *The Little Prince*.

> "It would have been better to come back at the same hour," said the fox. "If, for example, you come at four o'clock in the afternoon, then at three o'clock I shall begin to be happy. I shall feel happier and happier as the hour advances. At four o'clock, I shall already be worrying and jumping about. I shall show you how happy I am! But if you come at any time, I shall never know at what hour my heart is to be ready to greet you. . . . One must observe the proper rites. . . ."
> "What is a rite?" asked the little prince.
> "Those also are actions too often neglected," said the fox. "They are what makes one day different from other days, one hour from other hours." [p. 68]

The value of rituals is realized by many parents who establish special ways of relating with their children—rituals that contain a unique flavor no matter how often they are repeated or how crazy they may appear to others. Rituals can continue to hold a particular meaning into adulthood and old age, adding zest, enthusiasm, spirit, and life, to meetings with significant others. Some activities in which rituals may be created and sustained throughout life are story telling, reading poetry, painting together, listening to music, lying quietly side by side, taking a walk, dancing creatively, preparing and sharing special foods, setting aside a regular time to be together, writing special messages, and creating unique names for each other.

One of the most magnificent experiences I have ever had in therapy was with Barbara, diagnosed as schizophrenic (Moustakas 1981). Since early childhood she had been humiliated, taunted, and called hunchback because of a severe spinal curvature. My usual ways of beginning therapy were ineffective. She sat quietly, silently, numb to nearly all of my interventions. One day she arrived looking weary and unhappy. She asked for a cup of tea.

From this simple request a process of therapy was initiated that resembled a Japanese tea ceremony—a series of rituals each containing a special and unique meaning, beginning with the quiet preparations and culminating in the slow, savoring drinking of the tea. At these times, when Barbara spoke, her words were not edgy or agitated. She communicated different aspects of her life and described her relations with the people she encountered during the week. On the whole she lived as a recluse and rarely left her home. Our weekly meetings became the pivotal point of her life. In mysterious ways our rituals awakened her, and she began having regular contacts with others in her neighborhood.

The tea ceremony was the center of our world. I often sat with her entranced as she gently spoke of the events of the week, presenting them in the form of a gazette but without the usual linking words and connecting phrases. In simple, poignant expressions, she spoke of current and pending activities. She had not lost touch with tenderness or with simple values; each event was like a treasure for her; she enjoyed each act, each vision of reality, noticing a blade of grass, watching the movement of a cloud, savoring the flavor and warmth of our growing communion. When she came, my office seemed alive with spirits, and strange moods filled the atmosphere. Often with her I experienced a distinct feeling of joy, a kind of levity and light, a sense of tranquility (no matter how frustrating or busy my life had been). Our rituals brought me a feeling of peace and contentment. Sometimes we engaged in private reveries or meditated. We began our meetings in the darkness of the world she brought with her, but very quickly we merged into the sunlight. Something in her presence touched off something unique in me, and a feeling of wonder was created. Our meeting room became a sanctuary.

As I have indicated, most of our life together revolved around the tea ceremony, but our meetings always ended with a music experience. Experimental surgery aimed at correcting a back deformity had caused extensive brain damage and destroyed most of Barbara's cognitive skills. She no longer wrote or spoke in the usual ways; she did not read in ordinary ways; most of her communications were atypical, and she could be understood and appreciated only through the medium of the ritual. I came to value these vivid words and shorthand expressions; just one of her words was a sudden bursting through of life. Everything from her past had been altered or severed, but somehow she had maintained her connection as a talented pianist. One day following the tea ceremony, Barbara expressed a desire to play for me. From this time, with each visit she brought a different selection, usually of classical music, and we ended each session in the same way—with a music experience. As Barbara played exquisitely, we entered into a kind of trance, and when the music was finished, we walked lightly, with renewed energy and optimism. Barbara left ready to face the world again, uplifted and feeling great. The unique pattern of our life together, the continuity and sameness, came to have value and meaning.

In *Rituals in Families and Family Therapy* (Imber-Black et al. 1988), four constituents are outlined as comprising the key aspects of ritual:

1. *Repetition*—not necessarily just in action but also of content and form.
2. *Acting*—not just saying or thinking something but also doing something.
3. *Special behavior or stylization*—where behaviors and symbols are set apart from their usual common uses.
4. *Order*—some beginning and end and containment for spontaneity.
5. *Evocative presentational style*—where through staging and focus an "attentive state of mind" is created.
6. *Collective dimension*—where there is social meaning. [p. 7]

## RECEPTIVITY, ATTUNEMENT, AND BODYING FORTH

To be receptive to another human being who is struggling to find a way to live means to be present, to be open, to listen with love, and to hear and receive whatever manifests itself, whatever appears in the consciousness of the other, to let what is be and in its being disclose its nature. To be receptive means to let the other person tell a story in his or her own way, in its own process and unfolding. To be receptive is to provide a clearing, the light of a human presence that enables the person who is suffering in a relationship to find a path, to wander through the entanglements without being defeated or denied as a self.

When I am receptive to you, I accept you. I affirm you. Whatever you say or do is an opening or invitation to meaning. I accept your communications. I simply receive them. I stay right there with you. I continue to encourage your unfolding, even when your anger or fear are directed to me.

Receptivity is a force that I bring into the world of the other, a source of energy, caring, and light that enables the other to remain on the path of relationship, to gain strength to encounter the painful demons and to move forward. When torrential feelings are released, I remain fully present in being. When my communications are met with silence, I stay with the silence. My receptive presence enables, gradually, the sense of promise in relationship, the knowing of the meaning of unconditional love. The letting be of that which appears and is, is an essential component of the struggle to create a new life.

What makes receptivity a powerful resource in the struggle for birth is the *Attunement* of one self to another, to the other person's moods, situation, conditions, and ways. I experience the worry, guilt, fear, anger, hurt, loneliness, boredom, emptiness in such a way that this other person feels my presence, knows the impact of my face, posture, and being. I am attuned to the entire space between us, and all that surrounds us, all that is with this other person. In being attuned, I recognize and understand what the other person has experienced and is experiencing in the return and suffering that is within a relationship. I fit into his or her mood, atmosphere, and presence. The attunement takes on a validated intersubjective meaning, in silence or in words: "You feel my worrying about practically everything in my life"; "I see by the expression on your face that you really understand what I'm facing"; "You know what I'm going through"; "Sometimes it's like you are inside me, experiencing my feelings, knowing the intensity of my pain."

My receptivity and attunement enable me to Body Forth (Boss 1979), to be there in the world of the other, in the movements of the other, often before this world and these movements are disclosed. In a sense, I am there before being there. My body is ahead of itself, in sensing, intuiting, explicating, and knowing. In bodying forth, my body moves forward to greet you even before we meet. You enter my door, and, though I may be several feet away, you feel my presence right next to you. You feel my handshake or embrace long before we touch.

On a hot summer day my body moves to open a window; I feel the moving air before I actually open the window. There across the room, within reach, is the summer breeze. In a bodying-forth sense, the window opens before my hand turns the latch and pushes it upward.

*Bodying Forth* is an advance presence, an ahead-of-itself, that creates rhythms to support and encourage life and relations with others. In bodying forth, I create dancing movements that provoke, compel, and invite. Life takes on an energy, an excitement and flow, enabling a person to enter into relationship, lift out its old horrors, permit these threats to be, again and again, in lines, shapes, gestures, and words. Bodying forth is a way of motion, a way of being into the future, in a world of sensing, feeling, thinking, judging, like the belayer on a mountain climb who knows when to extend and when to hold onto the anchor. Bodying forth makes possible risking, looking again, seeing once more, projecting backward and forward in all that has been in relationship and all that is and can be.

Through the process of undergoing a new relationship, rhythms of Receptivity, Attunement, and Bodying Forth create a synchrony of feeling, thinking, moving; rituals that celebrate and honor I and Thou and facilitate the creation of a meaningful, incomparable relationship.

## BEING-IN, BEING-FOR, AND BEING-WITH

Three processes that contribute to the development of a relationship and enable receptivity, attunement, and bodying forth are Being-In, Being-For, and Being-With. I begin with my poem "Being-In."

Being-in transports me to the world of the other,
A sojourn, a dwelling,
In the presence of this other person, I listen to understand
And to affirm what is
Just the way it is, an internal entering into the other's world.

Emptied and purified of my own private thoughts
I am inside the other's feelings, gestures, glances
Fully present, abiding in the other's world in a sustaining way.
I hear the words, strong, clear words
     that express the pain and that point to possibilities that
     open pathways for a new and creative life.
Being-in touches the pain, goes through the
     suffering, realizes the struggles to live authentically and
     to touch the essence of relationship.
Being-in means *in* the other's world, connecting with what is
     and how it came to be,
Being-in is human presence; it means caring and acceptance
     of whatever is uncovered or disclosed.

When I am *Being-In*, I am totally immersed in the other; I
enter every expression, nuance, thought, feeling; every scene
or portrait, seeing it exactly as it is depicted. Being-In puts
me totally in the world of the other. My attitude and interest are focused on being aware and understanding the other
from her or his frame of reference. I do not select, interpret,
advise, or direct. I remain in the other's perceptual world as
a listener; as one who seeks to convey my understanding.
Often Being-In represents a new experience for the other and
is enough to enable a flow and unfolding that lead to fresh
awarenesses, that clarify and inspire the person to make new
choices, to initiate new behaviors and actions.

Being-In the world of the other person is a way of going
wide open, entering in as if for the first time, hearing just
what is, leaving out my own thoughts, feelings, theories,
biases. Perhaps Being-In in this pure sense is never perfectly
achieved, but it makes a difference when I enter with the
intention of understanding and accepting perceptions and
not presenting my own views or reactions. I believe that
when I deliberately enter into the world of another person,
in the way I have described, I am anticipating and directing
myself to just what is expressed. It is "as if" I am actually in
that person's space, inside that person's body, in that

person's world, and coming to know the person in a primordial sense. Such a process requires that I work on myself to achieve a receptiveness and open presence, that I set aside preconceived notions and convictions, that I prepare myself by emptying habits, thoughts, knowledge, and experience that would color the other's sayings, or that label and conceptualize, and that predispose me to make predetermined classifications of the person's character, personality, or behavior. In such a climate, being-in-the-world of the other facilitates new experience.

However similar the words of this other person may seem, they will be distinguished by textures and tones, by nuances and flavors, and by a wholeness that is unlike any other person's communications. Being-In is an entrance into genuinely knowing the other in her or his own depictions and portrayals, just as these are offered, unfiltered by my personal perceptions, judgments, or feelings. In the Being-In I want only to encourage and support the other's expression, what and how it is, how it came to be, and where it is going.

*Being-For* the other person is a different way of facilitating a relationship. In this process, I take a stand. I am in some sense *in* the person's world, but there is also a sense of our being together, in collusion. I am listening. I am also offering a position, and that position has an element of my being on that person's side, against all others who would minimize, depreciate, or deny this person's right to be and to grow. I express this position; the other knows where I stand. To some extent I feel the hurt; I experience the anger; I live with the suffering. I also know the joy of breakthrough; the feeling of an enhanced identity and the wonder of emerging self-esteem. For example, I may plan with a child how to work out a problem with parents or teachers. This Being-For promotes a sense of alliance, a feeling of being together in dealing with difficult situations. I thus become an advocate of the person with reference to his or her frustrations and problems in dealing with others. This sometimes has the character of you and me against the world. Being-For means directly and actively promoting activities and events that will benefit the other by providing opportunities, resources, and plans aimed at positive resolution of problems, in the direction of the person's own interests, preferences, and predispositions.

In contrast, although *Being-With* may include Being-In and Being-For, it is distinguished in that I am always present as an individual self, with my own knowledge and experience. What another person communicates enters into my own awareness and perception and through a process of indwelling leads me to form my own understandings, beliefs, and judgments. The Being-With the other person engages my entire being. This may involve disagreeing with the other's ways of interpreting or judging or presenting some aspect of the world. Being-With means listening and hearing the other's feelings, thoughts, objectives, but it also means offering my own perceptions and views. There is, in Being-With, a sense of a joint enterprise—two people fully involved, struggling, searching, exploring, sharing.

Indwelling is a key process in Being -With. Keeping alive my own imagination, I immerse myself into the other's account of an experience. I interiorize the experience. The focus of the other becomes part of my own attention and being and acts as a framework from which to derive additional knowledge and meaning. The thrust of indwelling is to direct myself toward meanings beyond the *appearance* of things, beyond the presented thoughts and feelings. Through indwelling, phenomena are centered, not as external objects or events but as pointers to meaning that exist inside the phenomenon or event. Indwelling is a conscious experience, an active phase; however, some aspects of it remain inarticulate. Intuitive visions, feelings, sensings go beyond anything I can record or think about or know in any factual sense. These aspects involve hunches, guesses, visions, risks, and spontaneous impulses. In Being-With, I become a searcher.

The glimmerings that emerge from the other person's communications offer beginning data from which indwelling clarifies and leads to a mutually derived understanding, pointing the way to resolve problems. Certain features in the problem-solving process cannot be specified. "They [clues] look like fragments of a yet unknown coherent whole" (Polanyi 1966, p. 75), and point to something beyond themselves. Clues appear and, when dwelled in, point the searcher toward discovery. Guides are present that keep the searcher on the path (Polanyi 1969, p. 134). Where the clues come from, and how the guides work, remains, to a significant degree, a mystery. In Being-With I enter into the other person's thought-feeling processes, dwell inside them, and come to understand and know that other person's world from my own awareness and understanding.

Being-With may also invite confrontation. The two persons, though fully committed and participating in a fundamental relationship, may at any point be on separate paths of understanding, in terms of what is essential to move life forward. They remain with each other, listening, respecting, and differing in their views and feelings. In the process, a struggle ensues; words and feelings are exchanged. I do not minimize or overpower the other person's judgment. I remain respectful throughout and on a level of equality. In the process, a new vision emerges of what is essential, and both persons shift in some ways their perception and judgment. In Being-With, the personal power of each is retained. Each recognizes the value of the other. The final perspective includes dimensions of both positions.

In Being-In, -For, and -With another person I am creating a unique and very special relationship, a new way of being-in-the-world with another person. The process may require that this person return to what has been festering within; and through the againstness experience—the return to the relationship in which the person was uprooted and denied—through the release of the old poisons or patterns, a new self is born.

The presence of another human being is often essential to the birth and serves as the inspiration for a person who dares to hope for new experience, a new life, healthy relationships in which one stands one's ground and remains an authentic individual.

Being-In, -For, and -With are essential ways of Being in facilitating a therapeutic relationship. To Be-With in a dialogic sense, especially in the process of establishing a therapeutic relationship, ordinarily is preceded by Being-In and Being-For. To participate in creating meanings with others requires that we create a life in that other person's world and know that world from his or her internal perceptions and views. Such participation also requires that we Be-For that person, supporting, encouraging, and taking a stand on behalf of that person's being-in-the world. Effectively undergoing the Being-In and Being-For processes enables the power and paradox of Being-With to come to life without endangering the strengths, resources, and competencies that have emerged, without threatening the relationship itself.

Perhaps ultimately in every healthy situation, the rhythms, the natural inward sense of I and Thou, guide movement and expression and determine whether a bond will be formed.

Hall (1984) points out:

> Of course, there are certain people who have a talent for breaking or interrupting other people's rhythms. In most cases they don't even know it, and how could they? After all, it's other people who are having the accidents, breaking and dropping things, stumbling and falling. Fortunately, there is the other kind of person: the one who is always in sync, who is such a joy, who seems to sense what move you will make next. Anything you do with him or her is like a dance; even making the bed can be fun. I know of no way to teach people how to sync with each other, but I do know that whether they do or not can make a world of difference in a relationship. [pp. 162–163]

In Anne Morrow Lindbergh's (1955) *Gift from the Sea*, the nature of synchronous interaction is vividly portrayed:

A good relationship has a pattern like a dance and is built on some of the same rules. Partners do not need to hold on tightly, because they move confidently in the same pattern, intricate but gay and swift and free, like a country dance of Mozart's. To touch heavily would be to arrest the pattern and freeze the movement, to check the endlessly changing beauty of its unfolding. There is no place here for the possessive clutch, the clinging arm, the heavy hand; only the barest touch in passing. Now arm in arm, now face to face, now back to back—it does not matter which. Because they know they are partners moving to the same rhythm, creating a pattern together, and being invisibly nourished by it.

The joy of such a pattern is not only the joy of creation or the joy of participation, it is also the joy of living in the moment. Lightness of touch and living in the moment are intertwined. [p. 104]

## CONCLUDING COMMENTS

In the context of the aforementioned values and concepts, relationship means new life, a new way of being-in-the-world. Relationship means going through a process of return, through the sickness and the suffering, returning to all that is festering within, through the againness of being uprooted and denied, and through the release of the poisons of old patterns in relationships, often in the presence of another human being who is in, for, and with the person who dares to hope for a new life. Through such a process, a new world opens and a new basis for being and relating.

Each unfinished moment, each unfulfilled relationship is a form of death. We die a little whenever we are not there or when we reach out to others and they are not there. The pain of broken dreams, broken promises, and broken hopes threatens our very existence, endangers our sense of self, our inner spirit that contains the seeds of life.

Then we must search for ways to return to what is fully human, to deepen our awareness. Often this awareness comes through focusing and through explicating the crux of what is happening. In a sense we must die within ourselves to be reborn and discover fundamental meanings of life, in solitude and in our communications and relationships with others.

# 6

---

# Freedom and Boundaries
# in Relationships

When I am involved in a significant relationship, I inevitably come face to face with issues of freedom and boundaries. These are values that enter my world when *I am impinging* on others or when they are impinging on me.

As an administrator of a graduate school, I am careful not to define freedom and limits of work and time for others. Even so, I am aware that, at times, the freedom of some individuals interferes with the rights of others. Thus, administrative policies are needed to support the freedom of all persons within the boundaries of institutional life. The determination of what is required is arrived at through dialogue, discussion, and concensus or compromise, the latter being an action of last resort. Limits are set only when necessary to achieve a harmonious balance in human interactions.

I believe that all interpersonal relationships—whether in the workplace, home, or society—face issues arising from the tension between freedom and limits. They affect how open or closed our relations with others must be. These issues arise not only in the workplace but also in friendships, marriage, and in all significant relationships.

## MEANING OF FREEDOM AND BOUNDARIES

Every relationship has resources for responding positively to the challenges and possibilities of freedom and boundaries. Freedom is essential in the deepening, intensifying, and extending of relationships, but freedom can also backfire, block, restrain, and damage life between people. In significant measure, the limits of a relationship determine which of its paths will unfold; freedom is growthful only in the context of limits.

Freedom to be oneself in a relationship is a way of being present, a way of being recognized and connected with life and with others. Being free means being at home with oneself, willing to disclose to oneself one's own immediate feelings and thoughts, moods, and internal states. Feeling free to recognize the presence of alternatives encourages one to make allowances for one's mistakes or failures. Freedom is the yardstick through which attachment is enhanced; it is the source of new energy and vitality; it is a way of being that enables us to feel just right about ourselves and others.

Freedom in a relationship lets me be, enables me to feel valued in my being, and sharpens my sense of who I am and what I believe. When my freedom is respected, I am able to view what I want or need as a legitimate force and striving. The exhilaration of freedom brings me into vital contact with others. The world is a good place, and anything is possible. I can become what I choose to be; I can explore and experiment, take risks, and know that my choices will be valued and that I will be supported in them. In freedom, my heart is guided by what emerges within me as vital and strong. Life with others encourages my most passionate thoughts and feelings. I am free to move off in new directions and to make changes in my life.

Yet, it is just this venturing forth, this spontaneity of being, this moving freely in the world, that inevitably brings me into conflict with others; that ultimately creates doubts, jealousies, resentments; and that threatens the security of my life. At such times, I become aware that there is no perfect formula to guide freedom. Unbounded freedom is a smoke-screen, a snare that draws people into its orbit, and then stings them in the most unexpected hour. We get caught up in illusions of freedom. We are absorbed by them, lost in our spontaneity, self-expressiveness, our desires and needs. Then the shock comes; the struggle begins. For the sake of peace and love, we may participate in a sham life. We may be willing to be moved into a host of activities with the "free" ones. We are often unaware of what is happening. Without the anchor of our own reality, as a center of our world, freedom is amorphous, spilling and spreading all over, pushing whatever or whoever is on its path.

## RELATIONSHIP WITHOUT BOUNDARIES

The dialectical character of freedom and boundaries inevitably evokes tensions at critical points in a relationship. A paradox arises: the only way to meaning in freedom is through boundaries. The only way that boundaries make any sense at all is through freedom. The paradoxical resolution enables both ends of an issue to be recognized in coping with conflicts of freedom and limits in relationships. The resolution through paradox enables each person in the relationship to feel free while bounded, to accept the limits of interpersonal life while also experiencing its freedom.

A relationship that ignores the boundaries of freedom severely threatens the meaning of give-and-take. A discontinuity results, and the participants struggle for power and control. One person in the relationship often succeeds in being the "free" one. He or she demands everything, directs everything; the other follows, serves, obeys. When the competitive strivings for power are equally effective, the two persons are at war with each other, both visibly and tacitly. When I am in a competitive relationship, I am pushed internally and externally toward purposes and values that are not consistent with who I am. When freedom and limits become an issue in my world, they usurp my time, energy, and thinking. Such demands contrast with the relationship in which boundaries connect me with my own self, with what I prefer, what I want or need, the way in which I can authentically express myself.

Freedom without limits in a relationship ultimately creates problems, casts shadows in my world, and throws me and the relationship into a whirl. Pure freedom threatens all relationships, disturbs their continuity and growth, and moves them into anguishing, distressing, and frustrating experiences. Two open and unbounded beings will inevitably clash, in styles, in perspectives, in preferences. Without freedom a relationship cannot exist, but without boundaries one will not know oneself or the other person.

When one is caught up in problems of freedom, in acting out and narcissistic behavior, or when one is stuck in problems that arise in being limited, a troubled relationship results in which neither person is authentically present. The persons, mechanically and compulsively, repeat what has been learned in the past. Previous involvements inevitably permeate current relationships, often restricting and distorting "the carrying out of inborn possibilities of relation to the world" (Boss 1963, p. 243). Boss (1963) states that in every actual relationship to something or somebody, the person's whole history is inherent and present. The essential questions are, How is it that the person is remaining, right up to the present moment, in a relationship that imprisons him or her? What is keeping the person in the same stuck place right now?

The way out of a destructive relationship requires a return to oneself and the establishment of new ties in which one is accepted in being and encouraged to develop one's possibilities, within the natural boundaries of self and other. What is required is the courage to stop being determined by others' behavior and expectations and to find within one's own interests and preferences the freedom and boundaries of an authentic self entering into relationships with others.

The boundaries of a relationship are its natural limits. When I recognize and accept these I am able to establish a genuine life with others, one that contains definite structures and patterns, limits of time and space, and markings of my own being. No matter how much I may wish to merge or fuse with another person, my own boundaries will in some way stand out and remain a durable reality.

## RELATIONSHIP WITHIN BOUNDARIES

Every human being is unique and is constituted in ways that distinguish him or her from all others. A relationship, if it is to deepen and grow, must be attuned to these differences, must recognize and allow them to be natural boundaries of I and Thou. I need to know my limits and the limits of the other person as realities in my everyday world.

The boundaries of any relationship are connected to the self of each person—interests, activities, bodily states, preferences, conditions of space and time, tempo and mood, the degree of desire for involvement, feelings, capacities, knowledge, and perception of reality, within the context of life experiences.

Since no relationship can integrate individual persons into a perfect and enduring unit, it is essential that each person find a path of solitary creation, one that does not diminish harmonious life with others. The boundaries of my world are more open and unfettered in solitary searches. There, I am free to explore and experiment, without need to consider or question the other's frame of reference, mood, or attitude. I can venture forth in a free sense, guided only by my own predispositions and interests. These are boundaries that hold promise for an expanded life, contours of my identity that add meaning to my actions and that facilitate my work projects. In such moments, I am bounded only by myself.

Although I experience a sense of satisfaction in my solitude, this does not constitute a full life; inevitably a yearning to return to a life with others awakens. The tug and pull of "being alone versus being with others" inevitably occurs and tests me. The challenge is to move freely from solitude to relationship; surrendering at times to myself, at times to others, and, in rare moments, experiencing the true and fundamental nature of I and Thou, in which freedom and limits blend into a perfect unity.

The call to others is inspired by the need for communion and love. Love enables me to believe that freedom is possible in a relationship, to accept its boundaries, and to rejoice in its being what it is. Separation from life with others into the wanderings of solitude brings new meaning to relationship. When the solitary is effectively interwoven with the interpersonal, freedom feels more free and boundaries feel less binding. As the freshness of relationship becomes less distinctive, the boundaries become more pronounced in awareness, and the need for solitude increases. At such times, I move less freely in relationship; I make fewer moves. I am more apt to pause and consider my thoughts and feelings before expressing them. I yearn for the life of solitude, where in an unrestrained way, I can once more find myself. In solitude, I am at home with myself. The boundaries of *my world* are more clearly identifiable. With others, I am more often aware of being bounded. Paradoxically, a life that includes intervals of solitude enables a relationship to achieve its continuity and depth. A commitment to relationship offers a sense of connectedness that makes being alone in the world a distinctive value, more powerful and more urgent. No matter how often one may fail to achieve unity in relationship, there is always the dream of mutuality, always the possibility of being alone and being together, the dream of a flowing harmony and unity of self and other.

## SOLITUDE AND BOUNDARIES

In my journeys to Greece, the path of solitude and the path of relationship were both strikingly present. Each had its boundaries; each offered advantages, supports, and limits. Traveling alone, I was totally swept into the colors, forms, shapes, music, tastes, and smells of Greek life. Everything had an unusual clarity and brightness. No matter how often I passed a mountain peak, a bakery, a tree, the seaside, each time I experienced a fresh and unusual beauty, nourishment, energy. I was called forth to new perceptions and new feelings. I experienced a grand aliveness, an inexhaustible vitality. Day and night no longer existed: life was infinite and timeless. I was carried away with visions and sounds and lived in a constant state of happiness. Greek words took on new meanings; they more easily rolled from me, as I communed with nature, ruins, and people. Everything was within reach; everything stretched out into new possibilities —being lost on unmarked roads; being carried into a religious procession aimed at cultivating and nourishing the earth; being thrown into a Greek church and suddenly finding myself chanting Greek scriptures; kidnapped, with consent, by a band of gypsies; and thrust into hypnotic dancing and fire-walking rituals. My whole life was out of control. Boundaries were fluid and expansive. Intimacies with people were immediate, whether in the city, on ferries, in the villages, on the hillsides or mountains. Each connection was an opening to new adventure. Since the limits were ambiguous, I often faced danger—dangling from a cliff top; driving to the edge of a road that ended in a deep chasm, being on a twisting one-lane, mountain road with a bus approaching from the opposite direction.

Yet, in each instant, boundaries emerged that made possible the moving on. Virtually every hour was one of independence, yet there were connections and natural rhythms that bridged every engagement of myself with others or with nature. Ultimately my life was filled by the infinite possibilities of time and place. Every space was open to unusual potential for being with others, without reference to anything but the moment and its concerns and requirements. Every experience involved a receptiveness and a bodying forth into the Greek world, into a life with village people, gypsies, shepherds, urban Athenians, reaching, stretching, floating rhythmically, into deep and varied sensory experiences.

I was continually aware of textures, weights, flavors, temperatures, visions, sounds, movements—all that mattered in a sensual world.

## COMMUNITY AND BOUNDARIES

My second journey to Greece involved travel with significant others, and immediately it took on a different character. Each person brought individual boundaries into every scene so that it became necessary to plan virtually everything—time, schedules, arrangements, discussion of how to share varying interests and how to compromise, searching for a common focus and direction, inevitably narrowing the possibilities for life. With effort to control the risk or danger, through organized, directed, sequential plans, the journey unfolded cautiously. The limits were exponentially increased so that virtually every major activity was bounded by multiple voices, urgings, needs, and preferences. Yet there was something vitally uplifting and beautiful in sharing the different facets of the Greek world—foods, music, movement, islands, and people—something very special in community that made sense of it all, including the accommodations and compromises that were a part of daily transactions.

Whether alone and free or together and bounded, whether alone and bounded or together and free, I found myself always returning to the opposite. The sense of fulfillment came in the unity of these processes, but it also came in being able to give each its full allowance, its own time and way. Remaining open to each pursuit and recognizing and living within the limits offered a rich and vital unfolding—a full sense of inner and outer values and meanings.

## PROMISES AND LIES

Relationships are alive and authentic when they respect the rhythms of both autonomy and community, of self-surrender and connectedness. They guard against deception, the lie and the sham. They remind me to be particularly alert to signs when my very breath is rooted in the breath of the other, when the acts I carry out fail to establish the limits of my individual reality. What is needed in such moments is an awareness of the attributions and expectations of relationships. I am speaking of everyday focusing and remembering, of an everyday vigilance that emphasizes understanding of my own being and the unity of being and relating. For the sake of peace, continuity, and togetherness, there is danger of slipping into the lie. In sharp and unequivocal words, Gurdjieff (1984) refers to what is required to avoid this abnegation of one's self:

> But you will see that it is not easy. And it is not cheap. You must pay dearly. For bad payers, lazy people, parasites, no hope. You must pay, pay a lot, and pay immediately, pay in advance. Pay with yourself. By sincere, conscientous, disinterested efforts. The more you are prepared to pay without economizing, without cheating, without falsification, the more you will receive. And from that time on you will become acquainted with your nature. And you will see all the

tricks, all the dishonesties, that your nature resorts to in order
to avoid paying hard cash. . . . You must stop inwardly and
observe. Observe without preconceptions. . . . And if you
observe this way, paying with yourself, without self-pity,
giving up all your supposed riches for a moment of reality,
perhaps you will suddenly see something you have never
before seen in yourself . . . that day in yourself the truth will
be born. [p. 7]

In a vivid and moving depiction, in a therapy hour, Laura
recounted the deceptions and lies in her marital relationship. She had come to realize that her life with Tom, after
ten years of marriage, was a fraud. She had never been a
real person in the marriage; never actually known her own
interests and inclinations; not acted on her desires to continue her education, to seek knowledge in literature, art,
and self-discovery. Throughout the marriage, she had been
an extension of Tom, serving his goals and responding to
his needs. Key people, with whom they had regular contact, considered their relationship an ideal one, but Laura
herself began to feel a restlessness and despair in her life
with Tom. She recognized the prison that she had built for
herself and knew for certain that she had become a victim
of her own deceptions. She was not the person Tom thought
she was. Nor was he the person she once thought. Accusa-
tions, recriminations, and attacks followed; the marriage
came apart and was dissolved.

The real burden began when Laura discovered her own
self, when she began to taste the meaning of freedom, when
she began to see the real shape and form of her world, when
she realized that she must begin a pilgrimage of self-discovery
and genuine relatedness. Laura no longer wanted flattery
and decorative communication. She no longer directed her
existence toward establishing a peaceful and secure life. She
sought excitement, meaning, and adventure. She was seized
by curiosity, pursued her own questions, and began to discover and develop a new identity.

The quest for Laura is at the heart of this appeal from Tracol (1984):

> If we are sick to death of the sham banquet, who keeps us here? Let's leave this table of deceptions and go together in search of real food. Let us, too, return to earth—return to the abandoned field of our own lives, and clear, plow, fertilize, and cultivate this unworked ground that has been invaded by weeds. And when harvest time comes, we will go and tell our other comrades how bread tastes that one has kneaded with one's own hands. [p. 25]

## PARADOXES OF FREEDOM AND BOUNDARIES

In considering the challenge of freedom and boundaries in relationships, I have come to recognize the paradoxical implications. When I am truly free, I am bounded, for being free contains within it a knowing structure that enables me to move without fear, without doubt, without anxiety. When I am authentically bounded, I am free, for I move within known limits, and within these limits I feel uncontrolled. My steps are my own. I am free to create my own rhythm, my own dance.

When I think of freedom, I think of my right to make choices. I think of the right of all people to choose freely. I have emphasized this in my relationships with people—children, youth, friends, virtually in all intimate relationships and in therapy. This quality has been a marking that many people have singled out in me—my encouragement and affirmation of this right for myself and others. I believe that to some extent this commitment to the right to choose has been out of balance. I have leaned to an extreme in this direction. In doing so, I have sometimes failed to offer the knowledge and understanding of my own experience, what I myself have recognized as realities in my life with others.

Several years ago, I came to a jolting awareness that choosing is only one component of freedom. My discovery was awakened through a brief letter from Wendy. She had expressed her appreciation for being able to grow up in a family in which individual rights were respected and valued. Then she inquired whether I had ever been aware of how hard it is for a child to make virtually all decisions; how, at times, she herself had yearned for my judgment or opinion regarding choices that opened before her. For me, at the time, freedom to choose was the stretched beam, the only truth. I saw from Wendy's letter that the making of *a good choice*, one that will promote well-being and growth, is as important as *the right to choose*.

## THE RIGHT TO CHOOSE VERSUS
## THE GOOD CHOICE

Since that time, the issue has created many internal struggles. After all the years of being dedicated to a philosophy of freedom, to a belief in the rights of individuals, I was at last faced with the challenge of developing a more balanced frame of reference. The insight seemed obvious, simple, and clear. Why had it remained so hidden through the years? Why had I been so careful not to influence the choices people made, putting my energies into supporting, encouraging, and affirming their right to choose? True, I had frequently observed the manipulations and the authoritarian actions of parents, teachers, and marriage partners. I had become overly passionate about freedom and human rights. In the process, I was missing a crucial component, the goodness of choices. While the right to choose is an individual matter, the making of good choices sometimes requires other voices and other judgments. I am puzzled still with how I held onto the "right to choose" so exclusively for such a long time when I had often witnessed the consequences of bad choices. More and more I have incorporated the freedom to choose within the boundary of making good choices. I have more often offered my own judgment, observation, and opinion. In such moments, I have felt much more unified, knowing that I had presented all that was in me, to be taken into account in any final decision while accepting the other's eventual choice. I have also sought, for myself, the knowledge and opinion of others in making decisions for my own life. I believe that this new understanding has resulted in wiser choices that have facilitated self-growth and well-being.

Several months ago, Stephen called me to discuss the making of a decision regarding a job offer. As we talked, he considered the advantages and disadvantages. I became aware of other factors—for example, economics, time, and distance. I also reminded him that jobs of the kind he sought were scarce. I reminded him that turning down a job risked lengthy delay in finding employment. I emphasized my perception of the realities; his focus was on choosing for himself. As we discussed the matter, I felt a sense of well-being in the offering of my reflective judgment and experience, while not imposing on his views. He was free to process and decide. Ultimately, he chose not to accept the offer. I believe that it was a good choice, that he had carefully considered the realities and decided that the position would violate his values and involve him in activities and directions that he did not support or believe in.

## THREE PATHS FOR CONFRONTING ISSUES OF FREEDOM

I continue this search with illustrations of three paths that are often followed in efforts to resolve issues of freedom and boundaries in intimate relationships.

The first example points to a deepening and extending of the value of a relationship while also enabling individual interests and directions. It involved a mother–daughter relationship and the struggle to shift from dependency to autonomy. Stella perceived her adult stepdaughter Ann as continually interfering with her life and making impossible demands regarding everyday choices and activities. As we talked, Stella's language was filled with descriptions of being repeatedly pressured by Ann, in ways that she felt were ruining her marriage. She believed that Ann was attempting to foster a dependency that she strongly disliked.

We explored the nature of freedom and boundaries and how these had influenced her development in other relationships. Stella quickly pointed out that she was much more fully aware of the limiting character of her relationship with Ann than of her freedom to be. I asked her to imagine how freedom might be developed both for herself and Ann in a way that would enhance the relationship, while not interfering with her own autonomy. After considering numerous possibilities, she settled on planning a weekend trip with Ann, during which she would share her feelings of constraint while expressing a desire for a new kind of relationship. Later, she reported that by opening a dialogue with Ann, each had an opportunity to voice grievances and that this cleared the way for the weekend adventure. In the process, they discovered some common interests; a beginning bond of trust was formed. Each recognized that they had a stake in the other's life. They agreed to be more alert to situations that might provoke rivalry and dependency and that would divide and separate them. They planned to meet regularly to create experiences that would contribute to bonding without denying their autonomy. By circumscribing the areas of involvement and resolving to meet within these boundaries, they set conditions for a peaceful and enjoyable alliance.

A second resolution in coping with issues of freedom and boundaries increases the cleavage, exaggerates the animosities, and inevitably leads to a stalemate. The energy in and between the persons is used to hold onto fixed perceptions, repeated again and again in the daily rounds of suspicion, fear, anger, and hostility. Everything is checkmated in developing maneuvers that alienate and isolate.

This was the situation described by Margo as she outlined the crisis she was facing in relationship to her father. Her father had departed from the family when Margo was 14. He divorced his wife and remarried. According to Margo, her entire early life with her father was marked by punitive rules, constant efforts to limit and restrict her, criticism, belittlement, and rejection. She felt that she had little freedom to be in the relationship. Since his departure from the home, possibilities for positive development opened, and she began to create her own identity. In his presence, major decisions were filled with anxiety, doubt, and fear of consequences. Slowly, over the years, she found powers within herself; she determined her own freedom and limits. As this happened, the relationship deteriorated, and a hostile, tacit truce was established between them.

Now, her critically ill father had requested a meeting— after twenty-five years of absolutely no contact. Margo felt that he had no right to make such a request; she did not trust his motives; she did not trust her own feelings. She believed that if she visited him, the scenes of her childhood and youth would be reenacted—his judgmental eyes would be on her once again, and his words would condemn her. Once more, he would determine what was to be in the relationship. He would pick at her and needle her. She had fought to be free of him, and now he was closing in on her again. As we talked, she explored the realities.

He was an aged man; he was critically ill, perhaps dying. She had not seen him for a major portion of her adult life, yet her perceptions and feelings were exactly as she remembered them in her adolescence. She had changed; she recognized that she was not the person who had left home over twenty-five years ago. She was clear about who she was and what she could do. As we talked, she came more into touch with her strengths. She knew that he no longer had the power to control her. Yet she was not clear about what to do. She resolved to remain with the uncertainty until she reached a decision within herself on whether to face him or decline his invitation. In the meantime, she was content to leave their relationship in abeyance.

In the third type of resolution, each person defines for the other the nature and extent of freedom and boundaries. Richard and Gloria had constructed a world based on joint agreement on virtually everything. They scheduled and planned activities that they would share together and agreed to the routines and duties that each would carry out. Being free meant circumscribing their lives with activities constructed out of a need for mutual security. Rarely were self-interests the basis for choice. The "togetherness" theme dominated their world, a world that was predictable and mainstream in every sense. Boundaries were determined by compromise, fear of loneliness, and the dangers and risks of standing out as an individual. Richard and Gloria lived in a marriage box in which few openings existed for uniqueness or independence of thought or action. They were free of any real challenges or creations; they were devoid of authentic identity and selfhood.

In therapy, the suggestion that individual pursuits might enrich the relationship angered and frightened them. They agreed that something was missing, that there were tensions in the relationship, but they believed they could be solved by more fully surrendering to each other and giving up selfish thoughts. Increased freedom for self-discovery would jeopardize the relationship and the marriage. What was needed was a more complete definition of boundaries; freedom was to be permitted only if it would enrich the relationship.

To summarize: Three ways that people meet the challenge of freedom and boundaries have appeared frequently in my experience with couples in therapy. First is a relationship that keeps open the possibilities for freedom and boundaries, one that recognizes the value of growing and deepening the relationship but also supports and affirms self-interests, self-directions, and self-activities; a relationship that works toward maintaining a balance between togetherness and individuality. Second is a relationship in which tensions and conflicts are chronic, aroused by disagreements regarding freedom and boundaries; a relationship in which one of the partners or both constantly strive to achieve the dominant position. In actuality, such relationships are often stagnant and stalemated, although externally one person may appear weak, dependent, bounded, and unfree while the other may appear to have unlimited power and control. Third is a relationship in which freedom and boundaries are defined by the need for togetherness, by a planned and shared life, and by viewing solitude and individuality as threats and invasions.

## AN EXERCISE FOR EXPLORING FREEDOM AND BOUNDARIES

A way of entering into "freedom and boundaries in relationships" is through examining the present nature of a core relationship, viewing it as it is, in its own reality. Once we can articulate and describe a relationship, we can begin to see its freedom and limits. Using Heidegger's (1949) perspective, freedom is "the letting be of what is" (p. 142). We must recognize the actuality of who we are as individuals and search for an understanding of the dialectics of freedom and limits.

As a way of approaching the issue, focus on a current relationship in which you have been worried, puzzled, and distressed. Such a relationship represents a challenge or problem in life and is worthy of exploration or search.

Consider the kind of freedom and boundaries that you would like to establish in this relationship, keeping in mind that genuine boundaries facilitate purposeful expression of freedom. Perhaps you must first recognize that you have departed from your self in this relationship; you have become estranged, removed from central dimensions of who you are.

The challenge is to find the dormant pathways within, to awaken what has remained unexpressed and undeveloped. Come back once more, to find yourself and be yourself. Move into the mystery that is you, and create a new awareness and discovery.

Seek first a major event, incident, or recent experience that clearly points to what worries and disturbs you in this relationship. Describe the incident or event fully, rooms, places, people, images, symbols, spoken words, and silent messages. Capture it in its wholeness, in all of its parameters or constituents. Return to the fullness of a moment of denial and alienation, of the loss of freedom and the distortion of boundaries. How did you feel? What were your bodily reactions? What words were exchanged? What remained unspoken? Were you aware of the effects of time and space? How did you feel as a self? What was your awareness of the meaning of this episode? How is it now in the return?

Make a list of activities involving the freedom and boundaries that you believe would establish authenticity in the relationship, consistent with who you are. Return to your self. Return to the relationship, with fresh perspective. Write a description of what the relationship might be if it recognized you, the structure of your being, the spirit, shape, character, and essence of who you actually are. Resolve to find a way to bring these new images and perceptions of freedom and boundaries into the relationship. Share your depiction with the other person, and enter into a dialogue aimed at achieving a harmony of individual freedom within the limits of the mutuality of the relationship.

**7**

# To Possess or To Be

In this chapter, I focus on what it means to feel or act possessively toward others, in contrast to accepting and valuing the being of others.

## NATURE OF POSSESSIVENESS

To possess is *to have* someone as one's own, like property, to control, dominate, and determine the direction of another's life; to dictate another's choices; to prescribe another's wishes, hopes, and goals. To possess means to take charge of; to decide and order what another person will do, how the doing will be carried out; and to dictate its value or lack of value. To possess is to analyze, interpret, and evaluate another person's ways, activities, feelings, preferences, beliefs, and judgments.

Many relationships, in subtle, indirect, and devious ways, and sometimes in open and blatant ways, involve persons whose purpose in life is to possess others, to have others in ways of living and working—sexually, economically, religiously, socially, and politically. In some relationships, one person strives to possess the other; in others, both persons battle to gain possession of the other. The marriage ceremony often in words, but sometimes tacitly, states "*to have* and to hold," thus denoting mutual possessiveness.

Whether one possesses others through sweetness, passivity, and indirection or through force, dominance, and assertiveness, the possession amounts to the same thing: power over others and manipulation and control of them.

To possess someone requires constant vigilance. In the possessing, one inevitably engages in a struggle of wills, resistances, and counterresistances. When we gain power over and possess another person, the person ceases to be who she or he is. A unique identity is no longer present; in essence, the person is no longer there. We end up possessing not the being of an individual but what that person has become under our influence, thus not the real person but a substitute. We may achieve ownership, but in the process we lose what is essential—the authentic person—for we can never own the being of the other as we own property. Yet, it is this particular being and not a substitute that the controlling person wants to possess. The being of the other remains inviolate no matter what we say or do. Even when we believe we possess a person as our own we do not. The essence of a person is not a possession, is not possessable. If we succeed in conquering the other, the other changes into a false or counterfeit something that is manipulable but that is not what we wanted in the first place. Thus, we have come to own what we do not want and to have power over someone who does not really exist. What does exist is a replica, a molded creature, but not the unique, original human being that we dreamed about. We do not own what we wanted, the core of the person as such.

The individuality of the other can be hidden and disguised, but it cannot be given away. The possessor can never actually *have* the being of the other person; thus, there is a disturbing loss in the gain. The loss goes beyond the failure to win the authentic being of the other—the possessor is also lost as a self in the process. In controlling the other, we lose touch with ourselves; we become a thing among things; an "it" among other "its". To put it bluntly, when we possess a person we not only lose the person but we lose ourselves. In effect, we use energies and resources to gain something that is not real, a manufactured entity, not the living human being. Not only are we mad in thinking that we have something that we do not have, but in our pursuit of that person we drive the real person underground. The possessed one has turned over only an outside or empty version of the real self. Each of the pair has driven the other into false identities, often without being aware of what has happened.

It is difficult to know when people are engaging in a process of possessing others because everything looks normal. Words and gestures may take on an appearance of altruism and caring while all the while a shaping, maneuvering, and molding is taking place. The external acts may not appear to aim at submission of the other and conquering of the other, but that is the goal. Everything in the relationship may appear to be healthy and in harmony. The everyday habits and routines have become silently binding, pulling the possessed and the possessor into a life of expectations and obsessive activities.

Being enslaved in a relationship, with all its fantasies and orderings, often remains unrecognized until a crisis occurs that evokes awarenesses of its real nature—the manipulations, distortions, and "shimmering" gifts. Everything appears in balance, until the possessed one, agitated by an internal and often unrelenting anxiety and distress, realizes that he or she has been taken over and obliterated as an independent self. Then the acts of devious manipulation and control that had been perceived as expressions of love are recognized as thwarting, constraining, and blocking maneuvers. The "honey" tactics are difficult to recognize. They appear to build up the other, but all the while the other is being treated as a property, and the proprietor is the one who holds the mortgage.

In possessing the other, the owner has lost touch with what is essential in being and relating. The possessor has also been dispossessed. The more one owns what one has, the more one loses what one is. This distinction between being who one is and being what one has is aptly described by Erich Fromm (1976):

> *If I am what I have and if what I have is lost, who then am I?* Nobody but a defeated, deflated, pathetic testimony to a wrong way of living. Because I *can* lose what I have, I am necessarily constantly worried that I *shall* lose what I have. . . . If I am who I am and not what I have, nobody can deprive me of or threaten my security and my sense of identity. My center is within myself. [pp. 109–110]

As Fromm points out, what I possess today I may lose tomorrow. I am forever threatened by this possibility and thus must be cautious, watchful, suspicious, and hovering in protecting what I have gained.

The possessor must keep a constant lookout on the possessed; this entails a continued use of energy and resource to keep the other imprisoned and to control the other's behavior and life. Such a situation makes for an unshakeable insecurity and a life of continual anxiety, in which the manipulated and the manipulator are locked together, irretrievably absorbed in each other. A leveling-down process takes place. Both persons are reduced to a minimal life, the hallmark of which is controlling and being controlled. Any innovation or new experience is threatening, requiring a whole new set of rules for programming the behavior of possessor and possessed.

The possessor may be able to trick the other person into actions that are not genuine or true, but ultimately the possessor pays a heavy price too in loss of potential self-growth and loss of an authentic identity.

Some people want to be possessed in a relationship. They throw themselves into the world of that other person, deliberately giving up their own interests, their own time, space, preferences, choices, ways of being, in exchange for the pleasure of being singled out and the security of being taken care of. Yet, no matter how much one may wish to be possessed and directed, no matter how much one may want to get rid of one's self, that self continues to exist as a haunting reminder of who one is, the truth of a personal existence. Always there are indelible signs that a personal, unique existence has not been extinguished. Something within the person will forever rise and torment the person to speak again as an independent self and to act as an autonomous individual.

The possession of another person is never complete, even when the person is not aware that she or he is being possessed. There will always be an inner restlessness that can break out in the most unexpected moments. This was the case of the woman who was kidnapped and literally kept in a box by a man for seven years. His power and control were effective only as long as she was completely in his prison. Her passage to freedom was to obtain employment. Since he needed money, he gave her permission to look for work. For a while his influence over her was complete, but a growing agitation against his domination eventually took over and she sought the aid of a priest. Her confession was aimed at helping her possessor, but the priest called the police and ultimately the woman testified against her jailer.

Control over another human being is never total. There will always be a flicker of self-light, an inner spark that may at any time burst into a flame and demand freedom of ex-

pression. Anxiety and suppressed anger will plague and torment the victim of possessiveness, until some act of libera-
tion is carried out.

For the possessor anything that interferes with complete
possessiveness becomes a threat—family of origin, siblings,
parents, work, friendships, special interests, or hobbies. The
one bent on possessing will attempt to eliminate all of these
connections. The threatening person or situation represents
a rival to be vanquished, either by subtle, indirect, and "loving" means or by the advantage of "in the best interest of,"
"for financial reasons," "for the education or well-being of,"
any powerful tactic that moves the one to be possessed, or
who has been, away from other attractions, bonds, or relationships. Undoubtedly, in possessing another human being,
indirection works best, the guise of altruism as "in the public's
interest" is a form of "I'm only thinking of you" or "This is
for your own good."

## NATURE OF BEING

Whatever the means, whatever the cost, however complete
the capitulation, the desire to be and being itself can never
be eradicated. An inner light will always exist and will find
its way to a clearing in some moment of crisis or sudden self-
insight; perhaps facilitated and supported by another human
being. To repeat, though a person may surrender to the possessive other, it is not the being that is possessed but only
external dimensions of that being

When we are in a relationship that accepts and values the
autonomy of being, we do not lose anything or give up anything or turn over anything. I am and you are; we are good
for and with each other. At times, we are together. At times,
we are one, but we do not surrender our solitary paths.

In order to love another unconditionally, nonpossessively,
I must be able to say "I" love; to say "I" love there must be
an "I" that is loving. For a loving "I" in love, anything is

possible. When I am loving you, I am loving myself loving you. I surrender my self freely, lovingly, yet that self is still whole, alive, and singular.

When another person invades our world and wishes to envelop us, to control us, to become possessive, it is difficult to stay on our own path, especially when we need love. To the extent that we are being taken over, we experience the darkness of a deteriorating self. We experience anxiety and guilt. We are selling ourselves for recognition, approval, and love.

What is often required at such times is an inward turn and, through self-dialogue and reflection, the recovery of one's powers, and the exercising of these powers to regain one's self. In renewal of being, one returns to what is immediately real, within one's own awareness. In being true to one's consciousness of reality, one is able to reach out to others, in the only genuine sense, with time and space for private thoughts and feelings and with desires for communion and connectedness.

Being, in an authentic sense, with another person, expresses itself in many ways, none of which are aimed at dominating, controlling, or directing. These include intentionally casting our gaze on the other, seeing with eyes that receive; committing ourselves with our own distinctive human presence; listening, accepting, valuing, giving, and supporting. We express love in a nonpossessive way by offering opportunities for extending the other person's choices and interests and by finding resources for our own growth and development.

## RITUALS OF BEING

In the process of return, a healing power is created, often through rituals. Rituals are openings for expressions of being. They are unique and distinctive ways of relating to others. Rituals nourish the life in relationships and instill it with a freshness and an originality. No matter how often a ritual is repeated, there is within it a spirit that is energizing and that brings to the relationship private and loving connections.

In considering rituals that are important in my world of phenomenal discovery, I search for ways that will distinguish and mark life with others. I am particularly aware of the rituals of freedom, the rituals of trust, and the rituals of will. In my experience as a therapist, I look for signs of *freedom* that might become rituals in my life with this other person. In the rituals of freedom there is always something fresh, something distinctive, something that will connect me with this other person.

I seek to create *rituals* of *trust* through which you may disclose in comfortable ways the secrets of your being and life, desires, interests, concerns, and troubles. I also am alert to moments through which I might encourage and support your expressions of *will*, patterns that you develop and pursue in making choices, in moving your life in accordance with your own timetable and readiness.

In the rituals of freedom, we create our own dance; our movements are synergetic. In these rituals, I encourage your self-directedness and self-expressiveness.

We *will* life into existence and give it its power and value. We choose our words and actions; we move freely and develop our own way to reflect on our communion. We offer continuity in ritual, yet each experience is new in how we feel and what we do. Ritual brings alive and vital meanings into our world.

In the rituals of trust, we begin each meeting with a recognition that affirms and supports us. You know that you will not be judged or criticized, that whatever you say or do will be received and accepted. You trust that I will be there, that whatever shifts may occur, I will remain with you. We may sit in silence; we may meditate; we may play; we may converse. What matters is that I am there with you, commit-

ted to your growth. You count on me. In time, these movements and presences take on a distinctive character that is
our own. No matter how often they are repeated, they will
hold fresh value in our relationship.

The rituals of will mean that we initiate, we direct, we find
a way to coordinate being. In therapy, I look for moments to
encourage whatever will ignite meaning in you, whatever
will bring you energy and life.

In van der Hart's *Rituals in Psychotherapy* (1983), a ritual
is described, following the reframing of an anorexia problem. What had been classified as a sickness is reframed and
viewed as a problem of fasting, a challenge that requires a
return to being. The therapist activates the will of Johanna,
pointing out that she has never really performed the ritual
of fasting properly, that the ritual must grow out of her own
volition as she moves to womanhood.

From that point, Johanna is in command of her life; she
decides on necessary activities. She acts on her own preferences and determines when the ritual of total fasting will
begin, how it will be carried out, and how it will be completed.

In commenting on the significance of ritual, van der Hart
(1983) states, "When the prescribing of a ritual was considered, the treatment had reached a dead end. The ritual broke
through the impasse, set Johanna's development in motion
again, and made further therapy possible" (p. 83).

The will rituals are the choices that a person makes, the
body movements and the language, repeated again and
again, not as ends but as processes that reflect that we are in
control of our lives. The stormy anger arises; violent attacks
occur. We punctuate our words and motions with them.
Scenes of pain and frustration are repeated, as are enactments
of releasing powers. These rituals enable the person to become stronger, to face fear with courage, to live through
whatever is troubling, live it again and again, go through the
suffering. In the process, the person regains control of life
and discovers genuine ways of relating to others.

Rituals facilitate and support communication. An alliance of being and relating is achieved that can face any adversity, a sense of you and me unconditionally facing life.

In ritual and ceremony, I connect with you but I remain fully myself. I do not possess you; you do not possess me. Neither of us is reduced in any way. Neither of us is defeated or compromised. We create something together or pursue something alone. It does not matter. Each of us exists in our own time and space, with our own values and meanings, and yet we find each other, within some definite pattern of communal expression; within certain values of caring, understanding, and acceptance. In this discovery of meaning is a distinctive bond that values freedom, trust, and will.

# 8

# The Dialectics of
# Teaching and Learning

Genuine education is a process through which individuals pursue real questions, issues, or concerns aimed at discovering, deepening, opening out, and extending their knowledge. Such a process involves passionate involvement, curiosity and puzzlement, and abiding interest. Carl Rogers (1969), in referring to the purpose of education, has emphasized the value of encouraging learners to charge off in new directions based on their own interests, concerns, and questions.

In this sense, authentic education invites connectedness to what is being learned, commitment and involvement between teacher and learner. It is person-to-person centered, an alive and active encounter between teacher and learner in which the natural power of learners to deepen and extend their own learning experiences is recognized and supported.

## WHAT TEACHING IS

I have been a teacher from my earliest recollection. I have
been a learner all my life. I enjoy and value teaching. In teaching I have learned how to teach and how to learn. I have
come to know the real meaning of helping others, the real
meaning of sharing ideas, of being a light and sparking a
light in others, of bringing hope into despair, courage where
there is fear, love in the face of hostility and hatred. I have
entered people's worlds when they have been in a state of
confusion, distrust, and self-depreciation. I have searched for
and discovered ways to uplift and affirm each person in his
or her own learning process. I have experienced a sense of
exhilaration and fulfillment when I could demonstrate a
method of creative discovery, when I could introduce the
value of reflectiveness and meditation in utilizing self-
resources, opportunities, and ways that would enable another person to feel, see, recognize, and know something that
mattered, something that opened new possibilities for
growth. I have witnessed individuals affirming their own
interests and powers, finding a direction, developing skills
and competencies, and growing in self-esteem and self-
confidence. Thus, over the years, I have increasingly prized
my life as a teacher. For me, teaching has been a way of learning, a way of expanding and deepening my own knowledge,
a way of expressing a life of commitment and relatedness to
others, a way of awakening to the numinous joy of sharing
with others in authentic learning processes.

I am in synchrony with Martin Heidegger (1968) who re-
gards teaching as an exalted activity that has nothing to do
with "becoming a famous professor" or "an expert in one's
field" (p. vi). Rather, teaching means being challenged to "let
learning occur." This can take place, Heidegger emphasizes,
"only when the teacher is more teachable than the appren-
tices, able to impart by his own example the proper relatedness to the subject matter being learned" (pp. vi–vii).

Thus, in a real sense, teaching is a calling, a way of being and living, a receptivity to helping others learn, a process of participation in the lives of others, a means of becoming involved in ideas, demonstrations, and experiences that will release and lift out potentials for learning, discovering, and knowing, a means of facilitating change and enrichment of the learner and teacher. These are my visions of teaching, and I believe that over the years, though not perfectly, I have remained true to these visions.

## WHAT LEARNING IS

I also have come to value learning as a process, a way of tracking that awakens, challenges, disturbs, and intrigues the learner. I have been alarmed by any learning situation that imprisons me, robs me of my rights and powers, and attempts to fix my mind with rules, facts, and memorizations. On the other hand, I have been ecstatic when a learning process invites and challenges me, when I am free to encounter and fully pursue an idea, issue, problem, interest, or concern. Such learning is worthy of struggle and sacrifice. It calls out my own purposes, values, and judgments, and respects my assessments. Such learning is rooted in exploration and inquiry that enables me to unearth what I need to know or what has been lost or concealed.

Learning is a way of pursuing what we care about, a way of fulfilling our dreams, a way of reflection and dialogue that moves us toward awareness and understanding, a way of invoking frames of reference that offer a direction, energize us, excite our curiosity, satisfy our urgings, and enable us to develop ideas and to create experiences.

Any education concerned with what is essential and enduring in learning recognizes the imperative of self-directed values and processes. In his book *Person-Centered Graduate Education*, Roy Fairfield (1977) has poetically depicted the nature of self-directed learning. In elucidating this basic value of a fundamental graduate education, he states, "by self-directing, person-centered learning, we mean the individual *directs self* (albeit with some help) along the path, along the parameters of identity and authenticity, amid the possibilities of speculation, into the valley of personal meanings" (p. 217). Such a learner, Fairfield concludes from his experience with more than a thousand master's and doctoral candidates at Antioch and Union Graduate School realizes a new sense of being.

Carl Rogers (1969) also has pointed to the necessity of self-direction in learning and has stated that learning is facilitated when the learner participates responsibly in the learning process, chooses directions, makes contributions, and lives with the consequences (pp. 194–199).

## SYNTHESIS OF TEACHING AND LEARNING

Teaching and learning belong together. One cannot exist without the other. To teach means that learning is present. When learning is present, there must be teaching.

*What* a teacher teaches will determine whether learners will be *present* to the teaching and present to learning. *How* a teacher instructs will determine whether a learner will be *open* to the teacher, receptive to the knowledge, and fully present as a learner.

When people who are called teachers are not opening up learning, they are teachers in name only. Teachers who mouth words that have no significance for learners are engaging in a meaningless process.

All genuine teaching is learning, and all genuine learning is teaching. Teaching and learning are bound up; they appropriate each other; they create each other; they influence each other; they determine each other's destiny and extend each other's time and space, so that teaching-learning is an encounter, a relationship, a continually creative happening (Heidegger 1968, pp. viii, x).

The distinctions that I have been pointing to between teaching and learning were clearly impressed upon me in my visit to Greek villages many years ago when I struggled to recapture the Greek language of my childhood. Among others, I traveled with an American professor who taught Greek at the college level. During my stay in Athens, she constantly corrected my faltering Greek, which faltered noticeably in her presence. She spoke for me when I was addressed by a Greek, in a way that stopped me from speaking. In her judgment, she was teaching me correct grammatical forms but when with her among native Greeks, I experienced insecurity, threat, and uncertainty. Finally, we left Athens and began our travels to Greek villages. In the very first stop, we were surrounded by a group of Greek peasants. They initiated a conversation with me. I hesitated to respond, for my colleague hovered nearby. Again, she entered the situation and communicated for me. The villagers did not understand a word of her polished Greek. She attempted a translation several times, and finally, in desperation, she turned to me to translate her words. It was a great and thrilling moment. The Greek language of my parents (who were born and grew up in a small Greek village) magically returned to me. I found my Greek tongue. They understood me. The intonation, accents, tone, and force of my words got through to them.

Looking again upon this experience, I am aware that it was not magic but the teaching presence of the Greek villagers that brought back my Greek tongue. It was their gentle, caring ways, and their wonderful body language, their receptive eyes and hearts. They encouraged me; they helped me form words that had lain dormant for many years. They waited patiently, supportively, almost lifting the words from me. We had a wonderful exchange over a period of two days that ended in rituals, prayers, fire walking, and trancelike movements and dances. My American colleague did not again attempt to teach me proper Greek.

## TEACHING-LEARNING CONNECTIONS

As a graduate student, my way of handling being placed in
a prisonlike atmosphere and forced to listen to lectures that
I had already read in the professors' published works was
to remain in the sterile environment as briefly as possible,
meeting the external requirements quickly. At one point, I
enrolled in seven courses—three of which met at the same
time. I went into the metropolitan community to find meaning in learning. I became involved with children, parents,
and teachers in schools in Harlem, Manhattan, the Bronx,
and the Hunter College laboratory school. There, I found
excitement, meaning, and vital ways of asserting myself,
developing autonomy, and trusting my own senses in developing new knowledge and in learning to deal with tensions, conflicts, and problems within myself and in relations
with others. I found ways to encourage self-expression,
locate resources, and facilitate creative activities in vastly different socioeconomic settings.

Another autobiographical event relevant to my own
learning occurred in my first year of postgraduate teaching of a seminar in interpersonal relations. At that time I
came to know and value the person-to-person relationship
in the teaching-learning process. I was in peril when I ad-
vocated freedom and the development of fundamental and
authentic relationships in the classroom. I had not been
aware that values and new ideas regarding interpersonal
interactions in the teaching-learning process were so threatening to the school administration's notion of discipline,
order, and role. Bringing ideas and ideals into real-life situations resulted in a lesson on school politics that marked
me as a troublemaker.

The seminar that I was teaching was entitled "Human
Relations in the Classroom" with the core theme of "Freedom in Learning." The superintendent entered my class
uninvited and announced that he had heard that I was pro-

viding teachers with a prescription for rebellion in the schools and in the classroom. He objected to my emphasis on freedom and demanded to know what I intended to do in *his* schools. I told him that my emphasis on freedom was not aimed at teaching rebellion but at stressing the value of interest, commitment, and choice in learning. I stated that denial of freedom in the classroom would push learners toward alienation and learning toward standardization and uniformity. He protested, shouting that freedom leads to chaos. At that point, I quoted Nietzsche's (1966) conviction that one must experience chaos to give birth to a star and Arthur Miller's (1987) assertion that every person has a star within and that one may spend one's life groping for it in bringing it to creative expression. The mention of Nietzsche and Miller threw the superintendent into a panic. He exclaimed that he wanted neither chaos nor dancing stars in his schools. With that proclamation, he left, slamming the classroom door as he departed.

I continued on my course, reaffirming that the birth of the star within is what teaching is all about, that teaching means letting learning occur, facilitating a process for discovering sources of life within and knowing that every personal star brightens world horizons. Once an inner self-light shines freely, it will never completely lose its luminous quality or its life.

In this seminar, I emphasized the crucial significance of the relationship between teacher and learner and discussed principles and concepts that comprised the healthy relationship. In such a relationship, the teacher offers resources, makes available opportunities, suggests options, points to possibilities, and provides information when this holds attraction and meaning for learners. In the healthy teacher-learner relationship, the teacher encourages learners to be who they are, recognizes, and values their choices, feelings, and directions, affirms their integrity, and supports their inherent tendencies toward self-actualization.

In the course of the year-long seminar, I asked each teacher to establish a relationship with a child, one who was irritating, difficult, withdrawn, or hostile. I suggested that the teacher initiate brief encounters with one child, at least once each day and keep a journal describing the nature of the interaction. Ultimately I gathered accounts of 92 of these relationships and published descriptions of them in my book *The Teacher and the Child* (Moustakas 1956c). A brief passage from one of these follows:

> This ends the contacts I have had with Ned. From a child who outwardly hated everyone, he has started to have successful experiences with others. He still has his bad days and slips back easily. But I feel much has been accomplished. I have changed in my feeling. I don't fight him anymore and his fights with me have stopped. I feel that he knows me and feels that I am an understanding friend who wants to help him grow. [p. 51]

In spite of the superintendent's opposition, I continued these seminars for twenty years, two more years in his school system, and with his support, as he discovered that what he prized in the teaching-learning process was not inconsistent, ultimately, with the outcomes of the classroom projects created by the teachers in the seminar.

To facilitate learning in a positive relationship, the first emphasis is on listening to what the learner is saying, entering into the learner's world of verbal and nonverbal communications. Such a teaching-learning process aims to lift out the learner's interests, ideas, and meanings. These ultimately determine how and what will be learned.

Without the fundamental human presence of the teacher, genuine learning is often denied or severely thwarted and restricted. The quiddity or essence of learning is what is sustaining; what grows, extends, and deepens in ever more complete layers of meaning. *Listening to* and *hearing* the nature and meaning of a learner's expressions are the essential qualities of authentic communication. Hearing the learner's own perspective and responding to that message provides the light that enables a learner to cross the bridge from mere memorizing and the semblance of learning to reflective thinking and creative discovery.

Carl Rogers has focused on three values that foster learning within a relationship. These values have been confirmed again and again in extensive research studies. The three values are *empathy*, *unconditional positive regard*, and *congruence*. All three depend on listening—sensitive, perceptive listening and hearing. Rogers (1969) illustrates this conviction:

> So the first simple feeling I want to share with you is my enjoyment when I can really *hear* someone. I think perhaps this has been a long standing characteristic of mine. I can remember this in my early grammar school days. A child would ask the teacher a question and the teacher would give a perfectly good answer to a completely different question. A feeling of pain and distress would always strike me. My reaction was, "But you didn't *hear* him!" I felt a sort of childish despair at the lack of communication which was (and is) so common. [p. 222]

*Knowing how* to listen means placing oneself in the learner's world. Listening means hearing *what* is being expressed just as it appears and responding accurately and compassionately. This moves learning to deeper and higher levels of meaning.

Gendlin (1972) emphasizes similar values:

> The point I want to make is that human beings are not machines that have loose wires in them or burnt-out tubes . . . that an ideal surgeon can reach and fix, or adjust, or take out the thing that is wrong or reconnect. . . . We are interactive, experiential organisms. *When* I respond to what goes on in a person, *then* something goes on *in him*. Of course, something goes on in him also before I respond. He is in pain, anxious

or dulled; he has lost his sense of himself; he does not have any feelings; everything is flat. When I respond (or let us say, when I succeed in responding, because I often try and fail for weeks and months), then something more is suddenly going on, he does feel something, there is a surprising sense of self. [pp. 333–334]

*What* a person is learning and *how* a person is learning are parameters of all learning. The *what* represents the fundamentals, the content that may be understood through sensitive listening and dialogue. Often the *what* is what the teacher requires to fulfill her or his responsibility and *what* the learner requires to make sense of and value *what* is being learned. Beyond *what* is the *how*—how what is learned is learned, how conditions precipitate, foster, and inspire learning. The most crucial factor is the support and caring of the teacher who guides the process. Again and again, in therapy, people described being blocked, criticized, denied by their mothers, fathers, and teachers. The shift to a new how in which self-esteem and self-confidence are precipitants to new perceptions and actions is inspired by compassionate listening and supportive responsiveness. Self-esteem is an ever-present inner light and can be called forth at any time by a perceptive and caring teacher.

In contrast, self-confidence is learned. It depends on recognition and affirmation. For this reason, learners move toward supportive people and away from people who judge and criticize.

The criticizing teacher is the witch portrayed in Jules Henry's extensive studies of classroom interactions. Henry (1963) points to a striking characteristic of American culture: the phenomenon of intragroup aggression, which finds its pathological purity of expression in witch hunts, where children not only confess their own evils but carry tales of the evils of others.

Obviously, in such a climate of learning, self-confidence is destroyed, and self-esteem is imprisoned.

Practically, as William James has stated, in the process of instilling anything at all of value in learning, a teacher must believe that learners will move toward significant learning when encouraged and supported. A learner must believe that a teacher will listen and hear him or her. In James's (1948) words, "Practically, that means belief; . . . there is some believing tendency wherever there is willingness to act at all" (p. 89).

What value is learning if the learner does not believe in what is being learned? Without belief, the energy and power of what learning is and means is dimmed, and no enhancement of knowledge occurs.

## STUDIES OF LONELINESS

At a critical time in my own teaching-learning process, through studies of loneliness, I came to affirm the significance of solitude, privacy, and individuality and the necessary awakening of self-awareness, judgment, and decision making in all fundamental and genuine learning. I saw how spirit gives breath to the words of the poem and the songs of the heart and how through the language of loneliness and solitude creative ways of learning are born. My studies of loneliness occurred in hospitals, in therapy situations, and in classrooms, and through them I developed a new research approach, *heuristic inquiry*. The heuristic approach is a scientific process that rests on the base of the tacit and gives meaning and direction both to intuitive and factual knowledge (Polanyi 1966, pp. 24–25). My immersion into the world of lonely and isolated persons awakened in me the desire to connect with them and be a part of their lives. It also led to a deeper understanding of health, pathology, and creativity and to the realization of the difference between the loneli-

ness of depression, despair, and alienation and the loneliness of creative solitude.

## TEACHING-LEARNING
## IN INNER-CITY SCHOOLS

Another transition in my understanding of teaching-learning processes occurred in the sixties, in my involvement with
inner-city Detroit schools. Cereta Perry and I (1973) developed programs that emphasized relationships, awareness,
communication, freedom, and responsibility in learning. Our
graduate students joined us in creating climates of learning
that recognized the learner's commitment, involvement, and
active participation in the learning process. We tapped into
children's stories; used their vocabulary, respected their language; encouraged their ideas; supported their interests in
music, art, and movement; and responded to their feelings.

Abe Maslow (1971) has emphasized these same qualities,
exclaiming that if education does not help a person know and
become who she or he is, it is useless:

> Education is learning what to grow toward, learning what is
> good and bad, learning what is desirable and undesirable,
> learning what to choose and not to choose. The arts, and es-
> pecially music, dancing, rhythm, art, and literature are close
> to our psychological and biological core. Rather than treat
> these as luxuries, they must be basic experiences in all edu-
> cation. [pp. 178–179]

Perhaps more than anything else what stands out for me
in the teaching-learning experience is the significance of
rhythm. In our work in the schools, we videotaped our sessions. We were startled again and again with the way in
which children came to relate to themselves and each other
in rhythmical patterns and expressions. We often opened our
sessions with a movement experience. As the weeks unfolded, the films showed clearly the synchronicity between

teaching and learning processes that had developed during a school term. Eighty children moving alone, moving together, moving randomly, at first in chaotic ways, and then, gradually, clearly, with harmony, balance, and unity, each person free and expressive yet connected and related to the whole community. This process occurred not only in creative movement but in virtually every learning activity in the classroom. It was the beginning of an awakening of the significance of rhythm in the classroom, the flow or energy and life from one self to another, the effortless way in which attentiveness, body awareness, focus, sensitivity, caring, and perceptual acuity connect persons in integral ways. Certain rhythmical patterns had the power to create bonds through the expression of tacit and alive capacities that were within each learner-teacher. They encouraged and facilitated our directions, interests, and desires. They offered support for well-being and participated in our unfolding. Edward Hall's (1984) *The Dance of Life* captures the spirit of what I am pointing to:

> A class that is going well develops its own rhythm, and it is that rhythm that pulls both the students and the professor to each meeting. What does it mean to love one's students? It sounds out of place in a university classroom, doesn't it? I am not sure it is even possible for me to unravel and identify the multiple strands that make up this particular tapestry. ... [W]e strive to bring out the best in each other and to somehow allow the rhythm of the group to establish itself and avoid at all costs the imposition of the artificial rhythm of a fixed agenda. [p. 166]

## CENTER FOR INTEGRATING TEACHING-LEARNING PROCESSES

The most recent transition in my teaching-learning process occurred following an announcement that the Merrill-Palmer Institute in Detroit, where I had worked for thirty

years, was closing. All faculty contracts, including continuing and tenure contracts, were terminated. Our degree programs in humanistic and clinical psychology, education, and
psychotherapy had been filled with maximum enrollments
every year since they began. A full quota of students had
already applied and been accepted for the following year.
The faculty in psychology decided to remain together rather
than seek individual appointments in other universities. We
believed in and valued each other; we knew that we had been
successful and that our programs had made significant contributions in the lives of individuals and in the community.
We approached the chief executive officer of each of five of
the most "liberal" universities in the Detroit area, hoping that
they would view our offerings and people as resources for
enriching their psychology departments. Each school looked
upon us suspiciously; there was no interest in the value of
our programs, only a concern for the money they might gen-
erate. The final blow came during our visit to the last school.
We believed that we had worked out a cooperative arrange-
ment only to be told that we would be expected to sign an
agreement through which our seminars, practica, and intern-
ships would be reviewed by a committee and revised to fit
the existing structures of the university. We terminated the
meeting quickly, dejectedly. We knew for certain then that
there was only one path open to us—to found our own
graduate school.

Through a series of intensive debates, maneuvers, gener-
osity with our own money, mysterious unknown powers,
and determined labor, we were able to obtain the Merrill-
Palmer charter and a building in order to offer graduate programs. We were able to open the Center for Humanistic Studies (CHS) in Detroit. The learnings, particularly the political
and economic ones, were at times harsh, discouraging, and
disillusioning. But something kept the energy and fire alive
within us, and we never lost hope. Through persistence,
concentrated effort and sacrifice, CHS Graduate School was

established. Its degrees are recognized by the U.S. Department of Education, the Immigration and Justice Department, the Internal Revenue Service, the Veterans Administration, the Michigan Board of Psychology; it is regionally accredited with the North Central Association of Colleges and Schools. Throughout the processes of obtaining these credentials, we did not alter our mission or our philosophy regarding teaching and learning. We did not revise our curriculum or our human values and procedures, nor did we waver in our commitment to each other and to learners. We have survived and continue to grow strong after almost 15 years of creative existence.

## CONCLUDING COMMENTS

The teaching-learning process recognizes the imperative of freedom within structure and boundaries; encourages solitude, relationship, encounter, and community; supports self-direction and self-evaluation; and values openness, honesty, rhythm, ritual, commitment, and caring. In genuine learning, self-esteem initiates the learning process; self-confidence enables it to reach a culminating place.

When I enter a relationship with a learner, I move with that person as an unshakeable spirit, staying with the power of unconditional regard until inner spirit and zest for learning are awakened in the learner. This can happen only when learning is approached with a passion, with a courage to pursue a matter in depth, with a determination to stay on the path no matter what. Sometimes this requires the encountering of boredom with madness, anger with dance, fear with drama, indifference with a persistent presence, until all the vital body parts are moved.

Only the humanness of the person at its core will touch what is untouchable in a learner, will reach the impossible. Often only imaginative visions and sounds will create a life that cuts through the deadness and awakens once more real learning and real love. This is something that is not learned by training or by sharpening of the intellect; it is learned by being open to human sources, by being transparent to life itself, by responding to the actual *rhythms* and shifts that are within every human being (Moustakas 1981).

Commitment to teaching processes that fail to recognize feelings that are inherent in every potential learning experience may be successful in teaching facts, but they may also kill the inner person, the human being inside. This was certainly the dilemma of the psychiatrist, Dr. Dysart, in *Equus* (Shaffer 1977). He could heal the rash on Alan's body, erase the welts, cut into his mind, take away his world of ecstasy, and send him puttering off into the normal world, and in that way turn Alan into a plastic figure. Dysart's realization of killing the passion in Alan was also an awareness that long ago the passion had died in himself, that while dissecting the heads of his patients, long ago he had lost his own head and had become a prisoner himself. With the pick in his hand, he not only had struck Alan but had destroyed himself in the process.

Without the rhythms of intimacy and passion, without a willingness to enter the imaginative creations of learning, to be inside the learner's world, in the movement of the senses, and in tangible thoughts and sensations that create new meanings, there is no hope that learning will be anything more than adapting to the normal world, to the ordinary and routine in everyday life.

I know clearly and fully that to move any human being in an authentic and primary sense I must touch, within the person, rhythms of that person's life, rhythms that will create a shift with reference to will, energy, and action. My challenge is to find the learner, to know him or her within the *moment* and to know myself within the relationship. When I enter in this way I create a bridge, a lifeline, a flow that fosters a single reality of harmony, meaning, and oneness.

Then suddenly, as it were, "a light is kindled in one soul by a flame that leaps to it from another" (Plato). We have all known dead feelings, dead ideas, and cold beliefs—and we have known hot and live ones. When a teacher-learner relationship becomes alive within us, everything else crystallizes about it. When teachers are really in touch with learners and accept and value them, when they really listen and hear what learners are saying, then children will draw from their own resources and powers and experience the freedom to learn.

Such an education claims the teacher and the learner, such an education challenges him or her to undergo an experience that enables genuine learning to occur and in Heidegger's sense (1968), "something befalls us, strikes us, comes over us, overwhelms and transforms us" (p. 57).

**9**

# Intervening and Anticipatory Caring

This chapter explores themes of intervening and anticipatory caring that have embraced my life with children in therapy and in the everyday world. In retracing the theoretical and scientific foundations of intervening and anticipatory caring, I revisited my books *Phenomenology, Science and Psychotherapy* (1988) and *Heuristic Research* (1990). I also reviewed my publications on child psychotherapy, including *Children in Play Therapy* (1953), *Psychotherapy with Children* (1956a), *Existential Child Therapy* (1966b), *Who Will Listen?* (1975b), and *Rhythms, Rituals and Relationships* (1981). I discovered that *Loneliness* (1961), *Loneliness and Love* (1972a), and *Turning Points* (1977b) also contained material relevant to principles and values of intervening and anticipatory caring.

Over the years, I have shifted from nondirective or client-centered interventions in work with children to phenomenological and heuristic approaches to psychotherapy which suggest ways of expressing anticipatory caring.

My initial journey as a play therapist began with studies and training experiences rooted in knowledge, methods, and practices aimed at becoming increasingly effective in employing intervening caring in relationships with children. This training first occurred at the Merrill-Palmer Institute in 1947 in a program directed by Dr. Amy Holway, whom I would describe as a humanistic behaviorist, educated at Harvard and supervised in treatment cases by O. Hobart Mowrer. From Merrill-Palmer, I entered Columbia University and studied with Virginia Axline and Nicholas Hobbs. I learned a great deal from both Axline and Hobbs about methods and procedures of facilitating therapeutic change and about the meaning and value of freedom and limits. For a short while, I employed a fairly consistent client-centered approach in work with children.

On completing my education, I returned to Merrill-Palmer to assist Holway. Unfortunately, she died unexpectedly before I was able to join her in Detroit. I faced the challenge of full responsibility for the play therapy program. I did not feel completely at home with either Axline's nondirective play therapy or Holway's humanistic behaviorism. I felt inhibited and restrained in these approaches. They were not congruent with my own way of being with children.

At times, I wanted to be more active, more directly a participant in the experiences of play therapy. I wanted to be more fully involved, to create with a child varied scenes of life, stories and images of what it means to face personal, family, and school storms and crises. I wanted to be with children in person-to-person encounters and confrontations and in ways that the models of my teachers discouraged.

At the same time, I valued the supervision I received and considered myself fortunate to be educated and trained in play therapy by two talented, incomparable women. Further, I could see from my own observations of their work that their interventions conveyed a deep, profound, and abiding caring.

Each, in her own way, watched over the children, protected them from further harm or damage, but left critical choices and decisions to the child. They consistently remained in the here and now of the child's communications in such a way that, as I observed their work, I often visually experienced what it means to a child to be understood and valued.

## INTERVENING CARING

I want to distinguish intervening from anticipatory caring. When I intervene in my interactions with children, I am interposing thoughts, feelings, awarenesses, and understandings. My aim is to help children recognize what is happening in their play and in their relationships with their parents, teachers, and others. I intervene to help children decide what they want to do, if anything, to change their behavior, reframe their perceptions, feelings, and thoughts and alter their views of themselves and others.

In intervening, I enter into the relationship in such a way that my presence is felt by the child. Intervention is an influencing force; its aim is to reduce the frequency and intensity of damaging or hurtful behavior and to encourage and support behavior that will be satisfying and effective.

My expression, comment, question, or silent response is simply a way of initiating a communication. In this sense, intervention is a kind of invitation without specific implications, motives, or desired effects. A positive intervention has meaning for the child; it holds power for opening or expanding his or her world; it points to another way of looking, consistent with the child's own interpretation. The intervention is an offering; if it fits, the child will use it; if not, it will be rejected. An intervening idea or meaning may be called up again at any time; a child can return to it and draw from it, when it is congruent with a child's own understanding, interests, or purposes.

Interventions have little positive value in the child's recovery of self-powers when they are not presented in caring ways. *How* an intervention is expressed is as important as *what* the intervention is saying to a child.

In the caring dimensions of intervening caring, the therapist responds out of having experienced to some degree the child's pain, tension, restlessness, or agitation. Caring conveys compassion, understanding, and regard. It is a way of expressing concern for the child's struggles, troubles, and suffering. To care is to attend fully, to heed, to feel some responsibility for, to want to protect from further pain or hurt; to watch over in a protective and supportive way, to feel compassion for the child's frustrations, conflicts, and failures. To care means to be with a child in such a way that the mutuality of I and Thou reduces the pain or loss. Caring means to enter the child's world, to understand the child's views, feelings, and experiences. Caring involves guiding the child in such a way that self-resources for positive change become available.

As important as intervening caring is in critical moments of child therapy, the most caring thing a therapist sometimes does is *not* intervene. At such times, the therapist is effective by attending lovingly to the child's unfolding expressions, being silently, humanly present. At such times:

> I want to feel what the child feels to the extent that this is humanly possible, to see and hear and touch in the child's way. I am totally absorbed in the being of the child, curious, alert, open, ready to enter any moment and be within the world the child is creating. I steep myself in the child's words, actions, interests, and concerns. My first intention is simply to know the child in his or her own orbit. Thus, my entire self, my energies, my life is centered in the child. [Moustakas 1981, pp. 49–50]

I encourage the child to continue to discover and create what is central in her or his world.

## ANTICIPATORY CARING

Although I have recognized the value of intervening caring and believe that I have become increasingly competent in making interventions that will facilitate the play therapy process, early in my experience with children in therapy I felt that something was missing, something from the roots of my own childhood. As a child, I not only learned to listen to others accurately and caringly, but I intuitively recognized underlying meanings in children's expressions that enabled me to anticipate what they wanted, needed, or hoped for and to anticipate ways that they might fulfill their desires, needs, and goals. From an internal source of tacit knowledge, I was able to point to openings that had not been seen or considered.

As a psychologist, the movement from intervening to anticipatory caring was gradual; it entailed a return to my natural ways of being with others, ways that I expressed with members of my family of origin and that were primary during my growing-up years. The caring that I began to express in therapy with children was conveyed as an anticipation of growth rather than as an intervening question, comment, or interpretation. I allowed my intuition to carry me forward to an understanding of an as yet unexpressed thought or feeling. I anticipated, in a caring way, the unfolding life of a child in therapy, helping something to happen—foreseeing a meaning, recognizing an opening, envisioning a possibility. Often I intuited something on the way, not clearly in a child's awareness but definitely present and unfolding.

Anticipatory caring is a concernful presence. It requires being with a child and responding in ways that are deliberately open-ended and unfinished. Anticipatory caring points to something in the future, not yet existing but taking shape as a possibility. In such caring, the therapist does not impose or push for things to happen but lets them be while also stretching or extending the boundaries of being toward

something in process yet not immediately present. Anticipatory caring supports the child's ability to become, encourages the child's freedom in decision making.

## QUALITIES, THEMES, AND ESSENCES OF
## INTERVENING AND ANTICIPATORY CARING

From an analysis of my prior research and writings, I
searched for principles, values, qualities, themes, essences,
and examples of intervening and anticipatory caring. I entered into a phenomenological-heuristic process, aimed at
discovering, synthesizing, and portraying the constituents
of intervening and anticipatory caring.

### Not Being Listened To, Not Being Heard

Of the many challenges that children face in their relations
with parents and other significant adults, none is more dev-
astating than the continual experience of not being listened
to, not being recognized, not being understood. Repeated
failures in attempting to communicate one's own feelings,
preferences, desires, and thoughts inevitably leads to painful and frustrating doubts about one's own competency and
value as a person. A profoundly diminished sense of self is
often the consequence of not understanding and not being
understood.

As a child's self-confidence is reduced by failures in
being heard, new avenues of gaining recognition are sought.
Attention-getting methods are invoked that do not represent
the child's real interests, attitudes, perceptions, or talents.
The child often produces behaviors and a style of communication, motivated by feelings of suspicion, inferiority, and
distrust. Recognition is sought through forms of withdrawal
or aggressive tactics. Often a battle ensues rooted in the
determination and will to retain one's power and authority
as a self.

The problem, which begins with a breakdown in communication and the failure of being listened to and heard, soon grows into serious distortions of who one is and who one wants to be. When that happens, children give up trying to say directly what they mean or what they want, yet the need for recognition and understanding remains.

When communication between the child and adult is on a positive, effective, human basis, they come to know one another and themselves. They clearly and freely exchange ideas and feelings. They share experiences and accept necessary limits.

Here is a striking example of a violent breakdown in communication between a mother and child. It illustrates the hypocrisy and the pain that occur when manipulation, deceit, and lies replace genuine listening and honesty in responding to a child.

Pottering dolefully to the room he shared with the twins, Ernie pried up the loose board (loosened by him) under which he kept his money box and sat down with it in his hand, wondering and occasionally shaking it a little. There were still in it two dollars and seventy-eight cents. Still thinking, he began to shake and poke at it to take out one of the coins, and presently one fell out into his hand. He stared. It was brassy; and then he wondered if it were a dream, for here was no American money, but the one-franc piece that he had often fingered in his mother's collection of foreign coins.... He shook and shook, in a frenzy, but with all the rattling, only the dream money came out, and as he shook out the last coin and heard that the light box made no sound but shook light as a feather, he became pale. . . . He heard a sound, made a quick dart to cover the money, and looking up, with a blush, saw his mother. With great hollow eyes she stood looking at him.... [S]uddenly his eyes filled with tears; he began to choke, "Mother, someone—" and broke down into miserable sobs. Henny looked at him, with hollow cheeks and desperate eyes, and in a moment sank to her knees, plunged her face into her hands and began to utter cries. . . . "Ernie-boy," said Henny unctuously, "don't cry: Mother will put all the money back."

"Will you," he insisted. "Will you?"

"Yes, dear; yes, dear."

"When?"

"When I get money: next week."

"What did you put that money in my box for, Mother?"

"I didn't want you to be disappointed, darling." [Stead 1940, pp. 413–414]

In this conversation, Ernie was left out in the cold. His mother did not hear the depth of his pain, the agony of his betrayal, the consequences of feeling unrecognized, not understood. These meanings are conveyed in the following excerpts from recent heuristic studies completed by Edna Earl Christmas and Matt Dickson, under my supervision.

When I experience the feeling of being left out, I feel flustered, rattled, self-conscious, awkward, uncomfortable, and out of place. I feel embarrassed and do not want others to know that I am apart, that I do not have a place, do not fit in, do not belong. I feel stupid. . . . I feel socially inept; and in some cases, I feel ignorant of group expectations. I feel excommunicated. At times like this, I feel powerless. . . . It's as though one glance from them is enough to waste me, to just hurl me backwards like a tornado. . . . I have the sense that everyone is laughing at me . . . and I just feel so vulnerable and exposed. I just want to slink away, cover my head, hide, disappear. I feel this swelling up inside, and I want to cry; but I don't want "them" to know that the tears are close at hand. I don't want "them" to know how much it hurts to feel left out.

Whenever I feel left out, I always think there is something wrong with me; that it's my fault; that I'm the reason I'm not fitting in and don't belong; that I'm different in some bad sort of way; that I'm not good enough. . . .

Sometimes, I am so angry. . . . I want to yell out and say " . . . how could . . . [you] do this to me? How could . . . [you] do this to me? . . . I don't deserve this. . . . I haven't done any-

thing to ... [you]. Why don't ... [you] care about me? [Christ-
mas 1992, pp. 78–81]

In contrast, a depiction of feeling understood follows:

When I perceived that you understood me, I immediately felt
an ineffable calm. ... Tension left me like a kinked telephone
cord unwinding. I felt a soothing quietness which permeated
the room. ... Someone had heard me. My anxiety was gone.
It was as if a raging storm had instantly stopped. ...
     I perceived a patience from you toward me. I felt no rush.
... I had all the time I needed. I felt no urge to force my words.
You seemed happy to listen. I trusted that you would wait
and still be there when I was ready to speak.
     When I knew that you saw what I meant, I felt safe. I gen-
tly lowered my defenses. I did not have to guard against you
or fight you off. There was no enemy in sight and I perceived
no threat. ...
     It was as if a black cloud had been lifted. My reduced shame
allowed me to accept my emotions. I no longer felt bad for
having my feelings, and they were no longer monsters needing to be hidden away. They seemed cleaner as if the green
slime had been rinsed away. I was now open to my experience
and willing to feel fully what was happening within me. ...
     You seemed to reach inside me and touch a faint spark
which burst into a warm flame. ... I had been tightly guard-
ing my secrets until your words melted the lock. The feelings
broke loose. It was as if their suppressed voices had been
screaming to be heard all along, but no one had noticed. ...
     I perceived your willingness to understand me as caring.
I felt that I mattered to you. ... I felt special and cared for. I
received the message that I was someone worth listening to
and worth getting to know. You noticed me from the inside.
[Dickson 1990, pp. 104–108]

## The Value of Play

Intervening and anticipatory caring are expressed by the
therapist in the context of a child's play. Play is a natural

means of communication for children. It is what keeps the child alive and in high energy. It is the spirit of the child in which creative life flows. To lose touch with the capacity to play is a form of numbness, removing a vital resource of self-expression and growth.

Play is a way of letting go, of thoughts and feelings that restrain, disturb, and imprison a child. Play permits children to immerse themselves totally in creative endeavors and to become one with whatever is taking shape within the self. Energy, life, spirit, surprise, fusion, awakening, and renewal are possibilities of play, openings and expandings for exploring self-interests and for developing the self.

A child robbed of the experience of unrestrained absorption in play, a child whose play has been made goal directed or achievement oriented, is on the road to trouble. When play expressions are blocked, the child loses contact with an essential source of energy and life. The child who is able to be lost in play retains ways of overcoming difficult situations. Again and again, I have witnessed children lost in the creations of play able to withstand the rebuke, rejection, and punishment. In this regard, I am remembering Tony who was considered a misfit by his mother and a retarded child by his teacher. Tony was able to move into an inner sense of play and create imaginative dramas that drew from his own real powers. Eventually, he communicated directly with his teacher and mother in ways that they saw his talents, and they came to view him as a precocious and inventive child.

## The Meaning of Therapy

I want to clarify what I mean by the word *therapy*. It is derived from a Greek word that means servant; thus it conveys the necessity of being present, being fully there. From this perspective, it is one's human presence that matters and makes a difference. The therapist's presence helps a child face difficult challenges on the way to self-discovery and self-growth, to being a unique and distinctive person, with a will to create life. This requires waiting for the child to choose to act, dare to pursue what is present in the way of interest and desire. This calls for unusual patience and an unshakable belief in the child's capacity to find the way, to come to terms with the problems of everyday living, a belief in the child's powers to listen inwardly and to make choices that are self-enhancing. Presence means receptiveness to all that is, readiness to enter fully and be part of all that happens, to recognize the child in the moment, without judgment, but with full support and unconditional valuing.

## Mystery as Process in Play Therapy

Another important theme of intervening and anticipatory caring that stands out as a horizon in my therapy with children is the recognition and "going with" the sense of uniqueness and mystery of the therapeutic process.

As a child I was fascinated by the deviant person, the odd one, the individual who stood out because of peculiar actions and interests. My fascination was not that of morbid curiosity but rather of wonder and of the promise of mystery, of entering into a totally different kind of relationship without any notion of what would be coming, worlds that almost always contained mixes of the frightening, compelling, exciting, and joyous.

I believe that responsiveness to the mystery of growth inspires children to pursue their own unusual interests and to stretch themselves beyond ordinary limits. When I listen fully to the spontaneous urgings of children or of myself I recognize the desire to explore new worlds, I locate energy and life within that radiates from intangible spaces, strange connections and associations that have no logical or rational basis. I believe that life is impoverished when we dare not venture where we have not been before, when we are taught to fear moving toward the undisclosed, when we remain always safely in the light.

What is crucial is most often hidden; it takes courage to face what has not been lived before.

I am struck with the mystery and wonder of discovering that the only way I can truly know another person is to enter that person's world, return to it again and again, immerse myself in it completely, in just what is there, looking, seeing, listening, hearing, touching, from many angles and perspectives, each time freshly so that there will be continual openings and learnings that will connect with each other, with prior perceptions and understandings, and with future possibilities. In other words, I must immerse myself totally and completely in someone, take in everything that is offered, without bias or prejudgment. And then in my own conscious awareness, thought, and presence, I must reflect on all that I have perceived and experienced—know again and again the wonder of another way of life, just as it opens and expands before me; know also, again and again, the wonder of my own conscious reflections that allow me to understand deeper and deeper meanings of the other person's experience. This beautiful connectedness between what is in the person, in its appearance and reality, and what is within me in reflective thought and awareness, is in truth a wondrous gift of being human. But knowledge does not end with such moments of connectedness, understanding, and meaning. Such journeys open vistas, but they are also openings themselves to new journeys for uncovering meaning, truth, and essence. This is perhaps the most telling reality of all, that each stopping place of our understanding and knowledge is but a pause. No experience is ever finished or exhausted. New and fresh energy is forever in the world and in us. When the connection is made and the striving comes alive again, the process begins again. There is no limit to our knowledge or understanding of another person. The whole process of being within someone, and within ourselves, and correlating these outer and inner experiences and meanings is infinite, endless, eternal.

## REVISITING BEING-IN, BEING-FOR, BEING-WITH

Being-In, Being-For, Being-With are ways of identifying the nature of a relationship, ways in which a person enters a relationship and influences the qualities and meanings that it embraces, its essential character. Being-In, Being-For, Being-With are processes that challenge, deepen, and extend life with others.

### Being-In

Conscious recognition, focused attention, and concentration of energy are skills that are utilized in understanding another person, the other's thoughts, feelings, behaviors, and experiences, as presented and articulated. Knowing another person involves steeping oneself in the other's world, listening to the words and the silences while also tapping into one's own perceptiveness and sensibilities in order to accurately understand and respond. The authentic presence of therapist to child is the hallmark of the Being-In process, a process comprised of methods and procedures that will guide, facilitate and enhance communication. Empathy and compassion are also essential in knowing the other, his or her frame of reference, goals, purposes, interests, preferences, and directions. To be effectively *in* the other's world requires that one be attuned to and receptive to whatever pathways of self-expression are opening. In the Being-In process, both persons evolve. They increasingly discover what constitutes genuine living, what choices will lead to self-affirmation, and what choices will lead to pathways of being and becoming.

Being-In is a pure state requiring that the therapist enter into the child's expressions exactly as offered. When I meet

a child in her or his being-in-the-world, I set myself to understand what the child is saying, or not saying, from the child's
presentations of self. In the Being-In process not only does
the child feel understood but the experience itself launches
new awarenesses of who one is and new ways of being-in-
the-world.

## Being-For

In Being-For, my task is to actively encourage expressions
of the child that will facilitate self-actualization. I not only
accept the child's offerings as communicated but I am clearly
and definitely present as an ally. I *am* for the child; I promote
our common purpose—the child's recovery of self-esteem
and self-confidence, and the child's learning experiences and
success in self-chosen activities and projects.

To Be-For the child requires that I make available my resources of knowledge and experience, my competencies and
skills for whatever positive goals the child wishes to pursue.
We become one in our efforts to find ways in which the child
can create a place in the world that is *for* his or her being.
My aim is to facilitate the child's actualization of potentials,
to support his or her unique and distinctive choices. In my
life with a child, again and again, I emphasize that decision-
making is within the child's own powers, a reflection of the
child's authentic voice. In Being-For, I do what is required
to enhance the child's well-being and to promote the child's
freedom to be.

## Being-With

The Being-With process evolves in the creation of an I-Thou
relationship between child and therapist. The process inevitably awakens numinous moments of life with a child, moments when therapist and child are together as a team, entering into the light of self–other dialogue and communion,

expressions of mutuality and regard, the valuing and enjoying of the sheer human presence of two people traveling on a common path. In Being-With, there is a deepening and extending of the bonds of relationship, a sense of equality, a mission that directs self–other purposes and contrasts of sameness and difference in style and form. In Being-With, a blending of knowing and being occurs, an integration of the child's incomparable, exquisite self-knowledge and tacit understanding of his or her own world and the therapist's professional–personal knowledge and experience of what it means to be an autonomous, independent person in a world that attempts to shape, mold, and reinforce patterns that conform to mainstream norms, that push children toward prescriptions of what is acceptable and what is required for success. In Being-With, therapist and child enter into an inimitable, sacred alliance.

In the context of Being-In, Being-For, Being-With, child and therapist create new rhythms. They move beyond the ordinary, safe, and routine and into a committed life. They dare to take new steps in inventiveness and discovery, to risk and experiment with new ways of being, and to locate within themselves new interests and new meanings that bring unique and distinctive qualities into their life as a whole.

To summarize, I have presented the following principles and values:

A set or intention, to enter fully into the child's world, to see and know what is there but also to let the child be, to recognize that every human being wants to change and grow but that each person's readiness and time-table is unique and unpredictable

Belief that within the child, however deeply buried, is an organismic wisdom that ultimately enables a child to make satisfying choices and pursue affirming experiences. Waiting is a key element in maintaining a belief in the forces of life that are within all children.

Intuition, spontaneity, the unknown—trusting inner guides, willingness to risk, realization that the intuitive is a critical power, in leading a child to what is vital in reality

Attunement to feelings and underlying meanings, often silent and unspoken, ultimately realizing that a unity of thought and feeling is essential

Commitment to life—no matter how many moments of frustration and despair occur; to persist in what breathes life into the child's world, what creates, inspires, and evokes energy and vitality

Active participation in whatever the child brings; response to the immediate moment in all its fullness, not holding back, being fully there.

When human values such as these are expressed and embedded in a relationship, they become the therapeutic agent that facilitates growth. They make possible the transition from one world to another, the transformation of a troubled life, the emergence of rhythms and new energy to create a healthy way of being in the world.

## EXAMPLES OF INTERVENING AND ANTICIPATORY CARING

From prior published reports of my psychotherapy with children, I have selected examples of intervening and anticipatory caring.

The first is a verbatim excerpt from my tenth meeting with Carol, an illustration of intervening caring (Moustakas 1956a).

### Carol: Intervening Caring in Empathy and Compassion

C: (Placing a clay figure that she has made into a vise). You put this in here. This is the last time I'm getting into this.

This is the only time. Then I'll forget about the whole thing.

T: Mm-hm. This is the last of it then.

C: (Still shaping the figure). Squawking all the time. I don't like that.

T: You don't want that, hm?

C: Squawk, squawk. That's all they figure. They just can't help it. Squawk, squawk. That's all they can squawk. Squawk, squawk. That's all they'll get back. If I don't get it, then I won't give it. I get squawk, squawk. Something else. That's what I'd like. Something else.

T: You wish they'd give you something besides squawking.

C: Talk, talk. Squawk, squawk. That's what they do. I'll put a snake in there. See if that squawks. Water snake, water snake. You go in there. I'm home, snake, and my mama won't let me go out any more. Squawk, squawk. Squawking all the time. . . . She bothers me every day. (Pause) It's so quiet around here today. That's what I want. Just so much peace and quiet.

T: That's what you want most. Just peace and quiet.

C: Because the old mother hollered at me every day. Hollered every day. And all she wants is peace and quiet. [pp. 130–131]

## Jim: Intervening Caring in Reciprocal Bodily Rhythms

Another example is derived from a session with Jim (Moustakas 1981).

For two days Jim had harangued his parents. All night long he had screamed about the accidental damage of a toy. He repeatedly harassed them with his demands that they find an exact replica. They had taken him to every toy store in their town to satisfy him, but each time he found a slight variation in the toy and his moaning and crying continued. They were unable to find a way to appease him. When he entered the lobby of my building the atmosphere was immediately

charged with tension. He and his parents were ushered into
a waiting room and the door was shut. . . . When I met him,
immediately he began his whining, screaming, and bizarre
communications. . . . Everything was uncoordinated and out
of harmony in a way that I had not experienced with him
before. I saw my task as that of finding him where he was,
connecting with his rhythms, not through words, but through
my own flailings that would reach and get underneath to
move us. . . . I announced loudly that it was time to go to the
playroom. Jim immediately bolted out of the door, screaming incoherently about his damaged toy. In every way, he
used his body to accentuate his derangement. The sounds that
came from him were so intense and shrill they filled the
entire hallway as we moved. His whirlwind motions were
like slashings, mutilations, smashings, . . . broken things
everywhere.

Finally we reached the playroom and I was about to suggest that in the room he could scream freely to whatever
decibel or range he could reach. But something stopped me
and I found myself imitating his movements (while adding
some of my own). He continued screaming a few moments,
then, all at once made a pronounced body shift and we were
in harmony. . . . I had found the pattern and together we revolved and gyrated in beautifully strange ways. . . . Soon the
whole room was silent. Jim was peaceful, and he began to
paint. The remainder of our meeting continued in this way.
When he joined his parents an hour later, he greeted them
quietly and calmly. They appeared stunned but accepted the
transformation and moved slowly out of the building. [pp.
13–15]

## Brian: Intervening Caring in Setting Limits

My meeting with Brian is another example of intervening
caring involving the setting of limits (Moustakas 1959).

Brian had been coming for weekly therapy sessions for almost
a year when his intense feelings of love and hate reached a

peak. For three months, he began each session with me with a sword and gun battle. He screamed with delight each time he "pierced or cut" me, each time he shot and killed me. When these battles were initiated, we had agreed to keep them within a ten-minute time limit. Following the battle with me, he would proceed to shoot and kill all human and animal figures in the room. He would take a rifle and scrape to the floor all items on tables and the tops of cabinets. Often he would open the plastic paint containers and place them at the edge of a shelf. He would shoot at the containers until the paint sprayed against the walls and onto the floors. This barrage and hostile attack had been repeated in similar pattern for thirteen weeks. Then one day we faced each other on a different interpersonal level.

The usual ten-minute battle had been completed but Brian refused to stop. He decided to use me as a target for what he called his "bow and arrow" practice. . . .

Mr. M:  No, Brian, I will not permit you to shoot me again. I'm going to have to insist that you give me the bow and arrows. (*Brian laughs nervously.* . . . He tries to pull away but I hold the bow firmly. He drops the arrows.)

Mr. M:  I'll just put these out of reach for the rest of this hour. You can play with them again next time you come. (Brian picks up a pistol, gun belt, and knife and throws them at me. I go over to him and hold his arms.)

Mr. M:  I can see that nothing will satisfy you until you've hurt me. I'm determined not to be a target of your attacks. If you persist I'm going to have to make all these things out of bounds for the rest of the time. (Brian laughs in my face as I talk to him. He pulls away.)

B:  You never let me do anything. All you ever think of is No! No! No!

Mr. M:  Yes, I know. You think I stop you at every turn.

B:  (Throws a container of paint at me.) I hate you.

Mr. M:  You have a right to hate me but I will not permit you to throw things at me. For the rest of this time this entire section of the playroom is out of bounds. (Brian is infuriated. He glares angrily at me, a cunning look crosses his face, and a sneering smile. Suddenly he begins laughing wildly. He throws the chalk and eraser at me. He tries to run to the "out-of-bounds" area. I block his path. He picks up a pile of books and throws them.)

Mr. M:  All right, Brian. Everything in this room is out of bounds for the rest of this time.

B:  You can't make me stay in this part.

Mr. M:  Oh, yes, I can. We've reached a point now where this is the only place we have. (Pause)

B:  I hate you. (Pause) I could kill you.

Mr. M:  Yes, you really want to hurt me the way you feel I have hurt you. (Brian slaps me.)

Mr. M:  I now must hold your arms. (Suddenly Brian completely relaxes. He lays his head on my shoulder.)

B:  You never let the baby have his bottle.

Mr. M:  You always had to cry and throw things before you were fed.

B:  I want my bottle.

Mr. M:  Would you like me to rock you? (Sitting together quietly on the floor, I rock Brian a few minutes.)

Mr. M:  It's time to leave now, Brian. Do you want to walk out by yourself? (Brian walks toward the door. As he reaches it, he picks up several items and throws them at me. He comes toward me and pushes and punches me. I take him and pull him out the door.)

Mr. M:  I realize, Brian, you couldn't hold to your decision. It's all right. (Brian begins to cry silently.)

B:  I hate you and I never want to see you again.

Mr. M:  But I want to see you again. I'll be here waiting at the same time next week.

Brian returned the following week. Having lived through an all-encompassing conflict with me, he began to verbalize his own feelings of self-doubt, and to relate directly for the first time numerous crucial experiences in which he had been severely denied as a self. In spite of the apparent breach of our prior meeting, Brian and I formed deep ties which enabled him to develop a new sense of himself and the freedom of honest self-expression. Brian is an adult now. He contacts me about once a year, comes to my office and shares highlights of his life. Occasionally he focuses on the challenges of setting and holding to limits. He remembers the battles we lived through but now views them positively and considers them a turning point in his own growth, as well as in his understanding of boundaries and limits in interactions with his own children. [pp. 17–20]

## Jimmy: Intervening and Anticipatory Caring in Coping With Death

This next excerpt illustrates intervening and anticipatory caring (Moustakas 1966b).

Jimmy's therapy started in a children's hospital one dark afternoon in a small room while Jimmy and his parents waited for the final report on a bone-marrow test that had been done that morning. As we played a game together, Jimmy was engrossed in moving the wooden pieces to successful completion, while I was very much involved in the meaning of the moment. I watched Jimmy. I watched the other children crowded into a small room, all waiting for examinations that would reveal their fates or indicate at what point they were in a process that would eventuate in death. Slowly, gradually, other children noticed Jimmy and me in the mass of people. They created a circle around us, and, feeling the invitation that came from us, they soon joined us in the game. The excitement of the play compelled the attention of many of the fifteen or twenty children in the room. A sudden quiet ensued, a stillness following the noise, as the children took their turns in the moves or watched as others played. The tensions melted, a calm atmosphere resulted, and the children played in a relaxed and enjoyable way, temporarily forgetting the ordeal that was to come, not even hearing the painful screaming of youngsters in the background, in the consultation rooms. But, I felt an unshakable sadness knowing the grief and tragedy contained in the room.

Thus, my first hour of "therapy" with Jimmy did not occur in the private setting of the playroom. Nor did we have the usual toys, materials, and space. We used what was available—a small room, crowded with children and their mothers. And we had only one item, a game, which we stretched enough to enable five others to play, a game that included many others who stood by and watched. Yet I am not speaking about a game. I am pointing to an experience in psychotherapy with children. These children found a way to live, to be active, to use their energies constructively, a way that temporarily alleviated the painful waiting and the terrible anxiety in facing the unknown.

The initial hour of therapy with Jimmy did not end with a game. The hematologist called Jimmy's parents. He wished to talk with them alone. Gently, he informed Jimmy that it would be necessary to give him a blood transfusion. Turning to me, the physician asked that I assist by remaining with Jimmy while he received the blood. In the meantime, he could have his private talk with Jimmy's parents in another room.

In this way, the second phase of my first "hour" of therapy with Jimmy began. I went with him to the special room. As we walked, I sensed his growing anxiety. When we entered the room and saw the bottles of blood, his body tightened visibly throughout, and a dark look of violent dread crossed his face. A shadow passed between us, a foreboding expression which spread so completely that neither my words nor feelings could break through this catastrophic moment. All I could do was stand by and wait until the first overwhelming swells of fear had subsided. After several minutes passed, in which Jimmy stood in a kind of paralysis, he recovered enough strength to get up onto the table, but his fear remained, and his body was tense throughout.

Getting the needle into one of Jimmy's veins was an ordeal. He screamed again and again. Unfortunately, the physician himself was unsteadied by Jimmy's reaction, and his aim was off the mark. He made numerous probings with the needle before he could make a successful entry into the vein. During this time, Jimmy's emotional state fluctuated between fear and extreme anger. Each time the needle stuck him, he yelled and jerked violently. The physician tried to convince him that the needle would hurt him only a little, but this infuriated Jimmy. He screamed repeatedly and threatened to get off the table. He demanded that his mother and father be allowed to come to him, but the doctor told him that his parents would not be permitted to enter the room until the blood transfusion had started. During this time, I held his hand and tried to comfort him. In words, I tried to tell him that I knew it must hurt very much. My attitude throughout was to remain with Jimmy, with his experience. I did not talk about the realities involved. I did not attempt to convince him that the blood had been ordered to help him get well. I did not explain the plan of treatment. It was not information he sought, but escape from this terrifying situation.

I did not believe that his fear and pain could be assuaged, but rather that he had to live with them, in all the intensity of his experience, before the severe, terrifying threat could be altered.

Finally, the needle was successfully introduced into the vein, and the flow of blood from the bottle into Jimmy's body began. I read to him during the transfusion, and, although he was still experiencing great fear, there were moments when the reading compelled his complete attention. He interrupted the story at one point to ask why the doctor had been so clumsy in getting started. I encouraged him to talk about this experience, and he expressed considerable feeling that the physician could not understand his fear or pain. Jimmy imagined changing places with him. He thought that the doctor would know how it felt if he could be pierced with a needle several times.

Soon after the transfusion began, Jimmy's parents returned. Their eyes were filled with tears, and their faces with grief. No words were needed to tell me that the tentative diagnosis of leukemia was confirmed. Immediately, Jimmy's mother took my place, standing by him resolutely, with an expression of determination and strength. For the next ten minutes, I remained with Jimmy's father in the corridor, trying to enable him to regain strength to be able to face Jimmy with the new knowledge that was as irrevocable as death itself.

## Barry: Anticipatory Caring in Visions of Creative Pursuits

My final excerpt is an example of anticipatory caring (Moustakas 1975b).

> With Barry, at some point in our second meeting, I sensed that art offered a medium through which he could express his feelings, and discover more and more of his creative talents. I added significantly to the number of art materials that had been in the playroom. I arranged them in a prominent and central place in the room.
>
> From our first play session, I learned from Barry that he had been engaged in a battle of wills with his parents but I also saw that he was determined to find his own way, no matter how much that way deviated from their preferences and expectations.
>
> In play therapy, his energy and behavior moved from the continual reactive fighting aimed at defending himself to engagement in creative pursuits in art through which he discovered his talents and the joy of participating in something of great positive meaning.
>
> Between his wars against his parents and his attacks on his baby sister, it was not uncommon to hear Barry singing, mixing paints and creating unusual designs with bright, vivid colors. When he was immersed in painting, he was quiet, deliberate, diligent in his efforts. At these times the tight, drawn face and the darting suspicious eyes changed radically. He became relaxed and peaceful. His paintings were a serious and profound expression of his being. More than anything else the painting process subdued his wild furies. In his paintings, he put his whole being, and he valued what he created in all its dimensions.
>
> As he painted, Barry came to understand and to know himself. He discovered what he could do and who he could be, and this discovery brought a special meaning into his world.
>
> The spirit that is Barry is still very much with me—the tough and tender feelings; the hard, dominant leader and the

soft and cooperative partner; the pounding, incessant willfulness and the receptive, enabling person, the loud, noisy,
and boisterous dynamo, and the serene and peaceful artist. I
lived with him fully in all of these dimensions, and my own
spirit rose on that final day when he left with confidence and
pride, carrying his last creation.

In his paintings, Barry willed to be himself and to become
fully a unique person both in his sorrow and in his joy, His
joy especially was passionate and shook everything in him
vividly alive. [pp. 53–57]

## CONCLUDING COMMENTS AND POEM

The encouragement of a child's freedom to be in a therapeutic relationship is inspired by the therapist's passionate commitment and caring, by a process through which new meanings and directions come to life. Such freedom of being for a
child is inspired by the therapist's unwavering integrity,
devotion, honesty, and love.

My therapy with children includes an awareness of myself
and my *real presence* as a unique being. This means saying
what I feel, being true to myself, no matter how much I may
differ from others, and regardless of the consequences. Regardless of how much we may want to take our cues from
others, we can only see with our own eyes and feel with our
own hearts. When we are not honest, we are not all there.
That part of us which, if expressed, would make us whole is
buried and a new, false, distorted image replaces the real self.
We are cut off from a significant resource, of ourselves, a vital
dimension that is necessary for unity and wholeness. A significant stream of inner life is removed, and until we recapture and know ourselves we cannot know other persons. The
authentic presence of the therapist, the consistently honest
and open communications of the therapist significantly influence everything else that occurs.

Ultimately, intervening and anticipatory caring are human
processes that affirm and support children and lead to the

recognition and valuing of their identity, growth, and ways of being in the world. The therapist within such values does not help out of sorrow or out of some professional role but, as Buber (1958) exclaims, "out of love, that is, out of living with the other" (p. 120).

This kind of helping involves sharing the suffering of the sufferer, bearing within one's self the child's troubles and concerns, and finding within one's own heart a way to lead a child forward, with courage and strength to become a person of self-esteem and confidence. What is required are expressions of love, as conveyed in my closing poem.

Love is selfless; love is tender, love is human power transformed into creative energy.

Love is the growthful substance of life; the delicate color and shading that imbues every hour, every day with uniqueness.

Love heightens our nature and being, inspires us, and creates a shimmering light that rivets our attention to what is authentic and what matters.

Love enables us to remain on the path of the other or to invade that path when our presence will support the other's growth.

Love holds a relationship together when it should be falling apart; love makes connections that cannot be severed except by love's departure.

Love moves us to invent and conspire, to engage in ritual and ceremony, to hold secrets, to make vows, to create magical rhythms and movements.

Love gazes entrancingly on the other, fuses a relationship and makes it whole.

Love makes possible the transcendence of mood and state of mind.

Love dissolves resistances and obstacles to growth.

Love removes the veils of self-doubt and despair.

Love alone heals a troubled heart and enables us to help each other find an inner light and rise again.

**10**

---

# The Impossible Dream:
# Visions, Hopes,
# and Realities

In visions, hopes, and realities, we are all explorers and seekers, free to stay on a path that is truly our own. We are free to pursue our capacities for ingenuity, invention, and innovation and to find new energies for actions that will move a dead and mechanical existence onto paths of meaning. We all have the resources to overcome obstacles and find creative expression for ourselves, even when opportunities are limited or when adversities surround us as we pursue the fulfillment of a dream. We are entitled to celebrate our existence. Each of us is free to go out into the world and create our own special dance. Jim Klee (1982) has emphasized that there is mystery in utterance, a subjective objectivity available to anyone who is courageous enough and daring enough to enter into genuine dialogue and become attuned to meanings within words and beyond them.

Connections between self and other, I and Thou, bring the dream into everyday reality and sustain our visions and

hopes of life's possibilities. Yet, despite the wealth of relationships, inevitably, harmony with others, mutuality of
purposes, values, and interests are splintered or severed. In
times of crisis or challenge, in transition, in the turnings of
life, we enter a darkness searching for crossings back to
where creative selfhood began and was denied or suppressed.

In such moments, the roads ahead are often blocked or
closed. At such times, I have stood alone, waiting for a new
opening, a glimmering or hope, a direction to help me move
ahead. A step forward has often taken me back to the place
where the unfolding journey ended, to a reality that had been
painful, to a relationship in which I had been betrayed, in
which trust had been shattered. In one such moment, a dream
of Binswanger's (1963) patient awakened within me a dream
of the rising and falling of a self that had lost the way.

> *Right before my eyes* a bird of prey attacked a white pigeon,
> wounded it in the head and *carried it off into the air. I pursued
> the creature* with shouts and clapping of the hands. After a
> long chase, *I succeeded in chasing the bird of prey from the pigeon.*
> I lifted it from the ground and *to my great sorrow found it was
> already dead.* [p. 229]

In my associations to this dream, what stands out is the
betrayal of trust, the sense of not knowing where the ground
is, too late to turn back, too early to find a solution, to make
a better choice. In such times, I have known the inexorable
death of innocence.

I have persisted, continued to search for self-resources, of
which Klee (1982) writes so convincingly in *Points of Departure,* aspects of the Tao, the turn toward simplicity, selfless-
ness, and the miracle that all at once alters the sense of the
dying within and the dying of the world.

At last, the painful thoughts disappear. I have faced the

full measure and substance of the loss. There is only silence, an almost perfect motionless presence, an inward surrendering, a pause, followed by a sudden ever-so-slight inward flickering. Slowly, I turn outward toward a new day, the new beginning of earth and sun. My body shifts its position in time and space. I have come into touch with a Kleean possibility, alive again in the loneliness and mystery of self-disclosure. I am moving from separateness to communion, from a private absorption to the intersubjective world of others. I have crossed the bridge from isolation to connectedness, from the doubting of my own sense of reality to trusting in the possibilities of a new world.

Once again I am attuned to the mysteries of nature, the falling leaf, the colors of fall, the winds, the shifting and wavering presences that call to me. To be attuned to such mysteries means that I must enter new pathways of self-in-world, become one with life—its jagged lines, its shapes, its invitations and uncertain directions. In mystery, things appear and disappear, fuse into one. Mystery unfolds in journeys along wide churning rivers, in near and faraway places, wherever there is the possibility of discovery, adventure, and surprise. In the middle of a dream, an idea is created, a new perspective awakens, a potent meaning emerges that will alter my life. In the mystery of myself, in the mystery of you, I find myself and you; we become one.

In the mysteries of a dream, a rhythm is born through which I participate in a renewal of myself, in novel configurations of shape, form, size, color, position, in the depth and movement of life itself. In the shifting seasons, changes in me are also underway, fresh patterns and thoughts awaken. I am able to speak in a different language. The raw materials of the dream bring waves of excitement, the possibility of unity and oneness with all that is.

I recognize, within the mystery of life, a home within me to touch and move. I dig deeper and deeper, to more elegant and essential layers of mind and heart. At the very bottom of my search, often there is no final answer. I accept the reality of the unknown in silence, the reality that I am on my own. I remain in the silence, at last embrace it. I am able to penetrate no further. I am held there in soulful presence. Neither reason nor fantasy enable a vision or take me home. I remain suspended in a universal orbit of doubt and uncertainty.

Mystery speaks to me in tacit ways, whispering secrets of life and death, pointing to vague and ambiguous possibilities, largely unrevealed. No further probing is helpful yet strangely, unexpectedly, in a covenant with silence a striking transformation occurs. Without explanation, the darkness turns to light; hopelessness points the way to courage; life takes on a new determination. A door opens again; the path is inviting; intimate signs light up along the way.

Mystery offers an opportunity for change: it induces unknown powers at work within us and in the world, forces that turn the impossible dream toward glimmerings within the self; an inward key unlocks the prison and brings a renewal of hope, often only in fragments at first, but ultimately everything is connected and in harmony once more.

Out of the darkness and the mystery that leads to self-renewal, the miracle of growth occurs again. I am inspired to return to life with others. They talk to me or sit in silence. I listen or speak. We create new perspectives, new awarenesses and understandings. The illuminating shift occurs because we have revealed ourselves to each other. We have disclosed the secrets of our world. We have encountered the mystery of I and Thou, in words and silences in the spaces in between, in deep down places, in inward churnings, in tacit ways and internal rhythms, in universal powers that transport us to new realizations of each other and the life we share.

A recent poem of mine (Moustakas 1994c) conveys the wavering rhythms of truth, reality, and mystery:

Truth, inherent in discovery, knowing
    reality in its own terms and ways, through
    explorations of heart and soul, in
    living with the other; In-being.
Truth, within a burst of tears, hope awakens within,
    determination, in finding oneself and others,
    songs awaken, lightning and thunder shatter old habits
    sounds and visions arise
    exquisite and unforgettable.
Truth, in searching, wandering, unfolding,
    deepening, expanding, touching,
    revelations of light and darkness.
Truth with passion, truth with heart,
    powers strong enough to push distortions aside,
    presences that sustain and radiate
    inside of being and in the world, at last a
    recognition of what is as it is, in its actuality,
    in its integrity and wholeness.

## THE MYSTERY OF THE UNFINISHED

Beyond the mystery of the eternal in nature, in myself, in relationships, lately I have been focusing on the mystery of the unfinished, the mystery of confusion and restlessness, the mystery of the unborn, and the mystery of the vaguely present, not yet clearly formed.

The unfinished in my life creates a feeling of being suspended, of being incomplete, of being unable to give myself totally to that which is. My energy is misdirected and trapped. I struggle to create a sense of unity. On the one hand is knowledge of my struggle, its sorrows and joys, and on the other the mystery that roots and uproots me. I experience the meaning, life rendering and deathlike, a sense of being fit, and the feeling of being an outcast. Will I ever know an enduring unity with others? With life? Will I ever reach a life of certainty in any relationship? An unquestioning trust? A perfect consistency and dependability? Will I always wander in the lonely night? These are nagging questions, uncertainties, fears, and doubts. What do they mean? What brings these questions to consciousness and leaves them hovering there?

No matter how totally I may surrender to some moment or how completely I may feel I understand something, or someone, in a moment of the restlessness of a sleepless night, what I see and understand holds a very different meaning. Within the unfinished relationship is the unthinkable thought that it will end disastrously or that its routines and repetitions will continue indefinitely. When a relationship ends, the mystery of what might have been follows me, tracings and markings of failed communion. I have lost something of life's invitation and possibilities; the tones and textures of my world have changed and will never be the same again. They have become subdued and shadowy; a relationship has ended before its time.

Unknown callings from within keep an unfinished relationship alive, agitated churnings of the self, the determination to find a path, to pursue an encounter to a place of closure. At one end of an unfinished relationship is doubt, frustration, disillusionment, and, on the other side, intrigue, fascination, hope, and vision.

I believe that we remain with the unfinished because of the promise of reward, of fulfillment, and our own will to see something through to its conclusion. An inner force supports connectedness, belonging, synthesis, a process that will bring a relationship to its deepest level, to unity, oneness, and communion. The mystery of the incompleteness of a relationship infuses us with a willful motivation to remain within it, to struggle with its ups and downs, its contradictions and its anguish, its promises and lies.

I am especially aware of the impact of the unfinished in my work as a therapist. I know that beyond the pain of transition, beyond the tears of inner dying, even beyond the anguish of an ending before its time, is the desire to know what the issues or problems mean, how they will affect us in the here and now and in the future. Nora, for example, had been struggling with the mystery of endings. In her talks with me, she moved back and forth, straining, stretching, sometimes creating violent and exaggerated movements. "I just want to go off into a corner and bury myself like a dog until I can face the world again," she shouted in a broken voice. "I used to do that when I was a child and no matter how much I tried to find someone, there was never anyone around, never anyone nearby." "I know how that is," I responded. She began to weep. "Why must I feel everything so deeply? Why me? Why must I be the one always to be singled out and left alone?" she shouted in heavy and desperate tones.

I too have asked myself that question: "Why me?" "Why is this happening to me?" I did not know what to say to Nora. My silence itself was agitated and restless, like her mood that suffused her world.

Nora recounted her story in unfinished sentences, broken off words, with increasing agony. Her daughter is growing up—she is moving away from her; she is losing her. She is unable to accept the ending. "We've been together only a short time. We were just beginning to know one another. What am I to do?" Her words trail off again. She is silent once more. The feeling grows heavier between us. All at once she stands up, moves around, stretches. Then, quietly, quickly she sits again, facing me once more, the tears still falling. She looks directly into my eyes. "Talk to me. Say something to me. Why must life be like this?" I did not know what to say— why some relationships remain incomplete, do not reach a satisfying fulfillment, why life between two persons must stop growing, why the everyday interpersonal life must end before its readiness and time.

I only knew that Nora's experience is not rare. The traces and reminders of unfinished relationships were strongly within me too. As she waited, in the silence, I spoke hesitantly. "There are some things for which we have no answer, no matter how hard we look or how deeply we search. You want to hold onto your daughter longer; there are still many roads to travel between you, dreams to fulfill, trials, hopes, and adventures. But that is not to be. You cannot control her life. You cannot imprison time. You cannot keep her with you any longer. It is time for her to move on to a life of her own."

Nora stopped weeping. We sat in silence again. She gazed into my eyes. At last something shined between us, a mutual recognition and caring. She smiled, "I feel better. I'm ready to move on to something else." We both rose simultaneously. We embraced fully and experienced the richness completely. I believe that the recognition and growing understanding between us, the simple, open sharing of an unfinished relationship, of unfinished visions and hopes enabled us to come together and find a way to a new focus in our meetings.

## THE MYSTERY OF THE UNSETTLED

The unfinished relationship undergoes the test of time and struggle. We enter into a state of impermanence with what remains unrealized. The unfinished leads us into the mystery of the unsettled, a restless period, in which the energy no longer needed for the unfinished is now available, but we do not know for what or how to work with it. At such times, we may give birth to something in a hurry rather than accept and live with the restlessness and uncertainty. To escape the insecurity of the unsettled within our life, we may jump into a new relationship before our time. There are people who go through life, refusing to live through the process of the unfinished, the unsettled, and the unknown, refusing to experience the tension and anxiety of transition, people who continually start new projects, and new relationships, without pause or sustained breath. Such people are tortured by the lack of definiteness, by the absence of activity and plan.

They refuse to enter into a gradual, timeless incubation process that precedes beginnings and endings.

The mystery of being unsettled must often be lived within a framework of confusion and chaos, sometimes with the madness of the insecurity of being, when there are no tangible, concrete clues or guides. Each mystery of transition holds its own unique twists and turns, tauntings and tearings, that must be accepted and lived with. Every unsettled time in life contains within it seeds of hope, a promise of a coming birth, the movement to fresh creations, a rainbow, vision, new love. As Linda expressed it, "The pain I feel when opening up again to someone or just to feeling and living again! I've shut off my feelings, stuffed them down. Then when I see the prospect of touching another person I have to open the door and I feel a flood of pain going into the closeness."

In living through the mystery of transition, in each moment, some element is revealed, but until the birth itself, the unfolding contains detours, risks, tentative reachings, experiments that come and go, until, at last, something seizes us completely and moves us through the darkness, toward the stretched beam ahead. In its rightful time, we can enter fully into a new relationship, in trust; then everything in life crystallizes around it.

## THE MYSTERY OF BIRTH

Out of the mystery of the unsettled, between the end of one reality and the beginning of a new one, a process occurs that, when followed in its own time and form, will lead us to a kind of death and then to birth. New life awaits within. When what is unfinished or unsettled is suppressed, it will insert itself again in some future moment. A quick birth created in order to end the restlessness lacks fiber, substance, endurance, loses something of itself, does not realize its possibilities.

Death that completes the unsettled in its rightful time opens a new path to life. *What is* is available and nourishes what is to come. The birth itself is genuine and can be savored in all its expressions and ways, moment to moment. The authentic beginning is mysterious and magical. It may be held tenderly, rocked in gentle rhythms, and gradually be brought into the light of the world.

When the mystery of birth follows its natural course, a whole new world opens. Within the process of creation, life itself becomes a mystery once more. Possibilities surround us, new pathways open, shapes and roads to ideas, and people and places just ahead, entirely new adventures, illuminations, discoveries.

The challenge is to let mystery be what it is in making choices, in pursuing adventures, in creating opportunities for what is and what will be.

At times, I have remained at the heart of such mysteries in my relationship with others, with their personal challenges and their struggles and desires to be. At times, the loneliness of being and world is overwhelming. Neither ordinary words nor silences capture the substance of another's life, or the gifts of self, in person-to-person ways. At such times, a poem is often a lifeline, a connection that would otherwise remain hidden and unexpressed. A poem offers possibilities that open pathways toward the birth of being. A poem can light up the world, and enable something heretofore undisclosed to show itself. Something is lifted out of its imprisonment and set free.

## Laura

The quiet way you walked
　　into my life,
Shy, silent, waiting.

When you moved it was with a power
　　that surprised me.

Songs of pain and darkness,
Tales of mountain streams,
Slopes rising in the sun.

Always, you came into my world gloriously
    with magical rhythms,
And a shining heart. [Moustakas 1987]

Without mystery life loses its most profound glories, the knowing of defeat, the spark of victory, the wonder of beauty, the anguish of suffering, pain, and death. Without mystery, the voices of the heart do not speak; the whisperings of the soul are lost forever. We need but open ourselves to life in all its forms and shapes of things to discover our own way of being, our own way of living and relating. Mystery is ineffable yet felt in concrete ways. Within every dream, mystery is awakened, the promise of life, hope for a future, the inspiration of renewal. We must learn to speak to mystery as it speaks to us. However much the darkness spreads, we shall find the light of our own being once again. We will connect with nature and the universe and once more connect with the real meaning of intimacy in relationships and the real meaning of life itself.

# 11

# Phenomenological Psychotherapy

# II

## Phenomenological
## Psychotherapy

Phenomenological psychotherapy grows out of my studies of transcendental phenomenology applied to my work as a human science researcher and psychotherapist, internship supervisor, and educator. Throughout, I will refer to individuals seeking psychotherapeutic insight and growth as the "person in therapy." The challenge of the therapist in phenomenological psychotherapy is to obtain "the completest and most careful description possible . . . of what is experienced by healthy or by sick people, of what is going on within them" (van den Berg 1955, p. 90).

The phenomenological model of psychotherapy is similar to that of the human science model presented in *Phenomenological Research Methods* (Moustakas 1994a). It includes the following processes: the Initial Engagement, Epochē, Phenomenological Reduction (comprised of Bracketing, Horizonalization, Delimiting to Core Meanings and Themes, and deriving a Comprehensive Textural Description), Imaginative Variation (comprised of Free Fantasy Variation and deriving Invariant Structural Meanings and Themes), Synthesis, and a Plan of Action. The methods that guide these processes are Informal Phenomenal Interviewing, Obtaining Descriptions, Deriving and Explicating Themes, Employment of Imagination and Intuition in determining the Existential a Priori, Developing a Course of Action, and Follow-Up. Each of the phenomenological processes and methods is presented in the context of psychotherapy and illustrated from interviews between therapists and persons in therapy.

## INITIAL ENGAGEMENT

In phenomenological psychotherapy, the encounters of therapist and person in therapy, from the first moments, create a climate that encourages safety, relaxation, freedom in communication, dialogue, and trust. These conditions facilitate free and open expression of feelings and are essential to the developing mutuality between therapist and person in therapy. The therapist sets aside preconceptions that would restrict an open meeting, "putting out of action" anything that would interfere with listening to and hearing what is being communicated. The following excerpt portrays the first moments of phenomenological psychotherapy:

> He did not settle comfortably in his chair but left some place between himself and the chairback. . . . His right hand, which on coming into the room he had kept under his unbuttoned waistcoat, removing it for a moment to greet me so irresolutely, immediately slipped back into its former position. With his left hand he drummed restlessly on the arm of his chair. He left his legs uncrossed. All this gave me the impression of a man already tormented. . . .
>
> His story amply confirmed this first impression. He was an undergraduate, but had not attended any lectures for months, because he could not bear walking in the streets in broad daylight. The few times that he had forced himself to

do so had remained fixed in his memory as a nightmare. He had had an ever increasing feeling that the houses he passed were about to fall down on top of him. The houses seemed to him to be drab and older than he had imagined them. They gave the impression of being dilapidated. The street had been alarmingly wide and empty and the people he had seen remained at an unreal distance. Even when a person brushed past him he had a feeling as if a great distance separated them. He felt himself grow unspeakably lonely and at the same time more and more scared. Fear forced him to return to his room and he would certainly have run if he had not been attacked by such violent palpitations of the heart that he had only been able to accomplish his return pace by pace. [van den Berg 1955, pp. 3–4]

The process of initial engagement is one in which the therapist encourages the expression of anything whatever in the perceptual world of the person in therapy. In the first hour, the therapist lifts out more and more completely whatever appears in the consciousness of the person, encouraging a full description, rather than an analysis or a mere recounting of events.

The Initial Engagement enables the person in therapy to be totally open and expansive in describing incidents, people, situations, events, whatever appears in consciousness, whatever points to the sources of pain, anguish, guilt, or suffering. Through the listening, caring, and supportive presence of the therapist, the person in therapy brings into the open whatever is relevant to the self and the world in which he or she lives.

As therapist and person in therapy work together during the Initial Engagement, the following challenges guide the process: (1) developing a climate that encourages trust, freedom, and open communication; (2) establishing the presence of concern and caring in the relationship; (3) releasing the person in therapy from the stranglehold of repetitive patterns and the anxiety and pain generated by destructive

188 Being-In, Being-For, Being-With

interpersonal relations; (4) shifting perceptions to the phenomenal world as the basis for understanding the meaning of things; (5) exploring fully the phenomena that appear in consciousness, looking at them freshly and naively; (6) accepting whatever manifests itself, describing its contents and its affects, and then letting it go; and (7) setting aside everything but one nuclear, overriding question, issue, or theme that will become the focal point of therapy.

Through informal, qualitative, phenomenological interviewing the therapist facilitates openness of expression and expansiveness of communication, thereby extending meanings and inspiring comprehensive descriptions with such statements as "Feel free to express anything whatever"; "Describe whatever enters your mind just as it appears"; "Let what is in your thoughts or feelings emerge"; "That's a heavy burden to carry"; "That feels like thousands of splinters of glass"; "Your anger is like a raging endless fire." Questions, such as the following, also facilitate the process: "What do you feel when that happens?" "Does it *seem* that that will go on forever and ever?" "Are you aware of being squeezed in on all sides?" "There are two parts to what you are concentrating on: what it looks like to you from the outside and how you are experiencing it from the inside"; "What appears when you look at the situation from the way others see it?" "What is your own internal experience?" Use of metaphors is particularly helpful in obtaining descriptive material.

To illustrate further the initial engagement, I return to van den Berg (1955). The person in therapy has just conveyed that his world has become terrifying and that he no longer leaves his house in broad daylight. Van den Berg (pp. 6–7) describes how the "emptiness , vastness, hollowness, and desolation" of space has drastically altered his world.

Such a view of space restricts one's world to narrow and closed-in spaces that will provide safety and security. Any attempt to cross over from narrow to widened expression might precipitate a total collapse. The description itself lifts out the feelings and the terrors. The therapist listens to the unique language of the person in therapy. Keen (1975) points to the nature of the challenge in the following excerpt: "I have to learn how to help her talk, and I must learn how to listen. The re-creation of her experience in mine occurs when she talks and I listen" (p. 34). In listening with openness and receptiveness and in the use of guiding questions, the therapist is able to guide the process. Language is employed that moves from explanation to description, from analysis to description, from a recounting of situations and events to a description of feelings, textures, shapes, colors, and sounds.

Throughout the Initial Engagement, whether the therapist communicates with statements or questions, the focus is on seeing things just as they appear, looking again, and yet again and again, with the aim of helping the person in therapy to describe the phenomenon more and more fully, from many angles and vantage points. In the initial phase the therapist seeks to understand just what is offered. In this sense, the process is similar to Rogers's (1961) person-centered therapy, as portrayed in the following passage from *On Becoming a Person*:

> I have found it of enormous value when I can permit myself to understand another person. . . . Our first reaction to most of the statements which we hear from other people is an immediate evaluation, or judgment, rather than an understanding of it. . . . Very rarely do we permit ourselves to understand precisely what the meaning is. . . . [I]t is not an easy thing to permit oneself to understand an individual, to enter thoroughly and completely into his frame of reference. [p. 18]

Phenomenological interviewing, in addition to employing the internal frame of reference, encourages and facilitates descriptions of experience. Description has the power to shift perceptions and meanings. The very act of describing is in itself something alive, something moving, an experiential way of viewing things that encourages understanding and change. When I can describe something clearly and fully, I have freed myself from the deadness of explanation and analysis. In describing, there is an emotional component, a spiritual factor, a shift in awareness, an alleviation of the stranglehold of repetitive speaking. Description is entirely my own. It is my way of looking at things; my way of presenting them, as they are; my way of opening myself to meanings. In contrast, explanation repeats itself; *what is* remains stationary, fixed; continuing on and on and going nowhere.

Description serves another function: it moves the person closer and closer to the nuclear issue; it helps the person stay away from the language of the past, from the everyday, from what demeans and robs one of integrity and life. In this sense, coupled with the value of free association, the Initial Engagement offers an approach to the problem that works toward freedom from prejudgment and bias.

The person in phenomenological psychotherapy learns that it is phenomenal reality that matters. Description is a way of entering directly into a phenomenal world of reality, a way of speaking to just the way things appear, from the vantage point of the experience itself, from the perspective of the person living the experience.

To summarize, during the Initial Engagement, the therapist (1) encourages free association to just what appears immediately and as such in the consciousness of the person in therapy; (2) guides the person in therapy through phenomenological and metaphorical statements and questions, aimed at lifting out and describing the phenomena that appear in consciousness both from the internal vantage point of the experiencing person and in terms of the person's views of how others perceive her or him; and (3) supports the person in therapy in setting aside biases and in abstaining from conditioned and programmed ways of looking at events, situations, self, and interpersonal involvements.

In a sense, the therapist is a researcher wanting to know this person in therapy from his or her own frame of reference, wanting to understand this person just as he or she presents herself or himself. In this sense, too, the challenge is to enter and immerse oneself in that world and come to discover the dominant meanings in this other person's life. At the same time, the therapist is a guide, aiming to facilitate openness, clarity and extension of what appears in the consciousness of the person in therapy, externally and internally; thus the therapist employs procedures that encourage textural descriptions, feelings, special qualities, time references, bodily concerns, colors, sense expressions—touch, taste, smell, sound, visual images—and features of temperature, weight, gravity or levity, density, intensity, and connections with nature, self, and others. The therapist's aim is to obtain a comprehensive description of the person's life world or life experience, who the person is in her or his world.

## EPOCHĒ

In phenomenological psychotherapy, the therapist engages in an Epochē process prior to every therapy session. In this context, Epochē means abstaining from or putting out of action preconceptions, theories, and ideas that would interfere with listening to and hearing the person in therapy from her or his perspectives and views. This requires setting aside interfering moods, attachments, and concerns that intrude on the development of an open and fresh relationship, that interfere with immediacy and spontaneity. Prior to the meeting, the therapist's self-dialogues provide a way to reduce or eliminate prejudgments, thoughts, and feelings that would predispose the therapist to view things diagnostically rather than from a fresh approach that seeks to obtain the meanings of life experiences directly and immediately from the person in therapy.

Epochē may also be necessary during the interview when the therapist's thoughts or feelings stray from the person in therapy and interfere with listening or when the therapist is explaining, interpreting, or imposing professional or personal views. The challenge during the Epochē process is for the therapist to listen to just what is presented, see just what manifests itself, support the descriptive explications of the person in therapy, and stay in the world and life of that person. The *horizons* of the person in therapy *are the focal points* for explication and understanding. Description is the method through which the horizons are explicated, through which a picture is constructed of the "what and how" of the person's world.

The Epochē process is initiated prior to each session and continues throughout therapy. From time to time, the therapist must remind her- or himself to look freshly, naively, receptively as new phenomena appear in the language of the person in therapy. It is also a process that can be used directly to help that person to practice a "clearing of mind and space," in Gendlin's (1978) focusing sense, so that each time the person looks, he or she is looking with new eyes, seeing something in a fresh and original way, a new angle or different meaning that contributes a more complete understanding of the experience.

Pat, a professional psychologist whom I was supervising, offered the following as an example of her effort to apply Epochē in her work with Sally, 28 years old, who had previously been in therapy for approximately one year.

On the day before my session with Sally, I wrote down the theories which I had formulated up to that time about her and her depression and its possible origins. I reviewed these immediately before seeing her, as a precautionary measure, so I would be aware if they began to influence my response to her and be more able to guard against their influence. I mentally reviewed these theories as well as other thoughts that I had formed about this client, prior to each meeting with her with the goal of being aware of and setting aside prejudgments that I might be inclined to make, and thus avoid making them. I was not totally successful in my attempts at Epochē and some of my theories did influence my thoughts at different times. I had formulated the theory, for example, that she is unaware of the anger she still feels regarding the death of her grandmother. In the next session with Sally this was the major focus. I believe that I caught myself before this impacted on my response to her, allowing her to tell her story her way, but it is possible that by verbal selectivity I might have indirectly conveyed my thinking. I did make an attempt to guard against this sort of interference.

To summarize, the Epochē process is an exercise through which the therapist refrains from bias by setting aside preconceptions that would interfere with receptiveness and accurate listening. The challenge of the therapist in phenomenological psychotherapy is to focus on just what manifests itself in the consciousness of the person in therapy, to let things appear as such, let them linger and reveal themselves in their own time, nature, and meaning.

## PHENOMENOLOGICAL REDUCTION

The next process in phenomenological therapy is the Phenomenological Reduction. Initially, this is a process of spontaneous, prereflective communications, but gradually it moves toward careful reflections on perceptual experience, judging, thinking, assessing, and choosing what is core and eliminating what is fringe or tangential. During this process, initial perceptions of meaning are corrected as the person in therapy delineates more fully what appears in his or her awareness or understanding.

The major phases of Phenomenological Reduction are Bracketing, Horizonalization, Delimiting Meanings, Deriving Themes and Thematic Explication, and Comprehensive Textural Description.

## Bracketing

Out of the Initial Engagement and Epochē processes, the therapy focuses on discovering the central issue or problem to be bracketed for intensive exploration, one that stands out in such a way that it is possible to see virtually everything else in terms of it. The challenge is to move this issue or concern out of its everyday context, its everyday associations, biases, preconceptions, habits, and routines, out of the usual way of viewing it, by placing it in brackets for focused investigation.

During the Initial Engagement, a host of issues, problems, or topics will emerge, but one will keep reappearing, or will appear with greater intensity, or will have a greater significance or impact in the life of the person in therapy. Putting this topic or problem in brackets does not change its content; it changes the way in which it will be reviewed, examined, perceived, described, and elucidated. The bracketed problem now becomes the phenomenon, the figure toward which all grounding of the person's world will be directed. The aim is to recognize it, let it be, let it linger and unfold. During this process the therapist obtains descriptions of the problem's many dimensions, aspects, connotations, feelings, and qualities, keeping the bracketed topic or theme exclusively in view, with sustained and unwavering attention. Should the person in therapy move away from the bracketed phenomenon, the therapist reminds the person gently of the importance of staying with the core problem. The center of attention and concentration, if therapy is to progress, is the bracketed issue or problem.

Of course, what is bracketed may shift in value. What at first appears central when looked at more closely may turn out to be peripheral; what has been peripheral on reconsideration may come to be paramount. There may be many changes before the bracketed phenomenon is held to and persists as the central issue, concern, or problem that dominates the person's consciousness.

In one situation, the person in therapy, Stella, bracketed "being criticized" as the major source of her trouble, but as her feelings were explored, it became clear to her that what brought misery into her relationships with others was not being critized but rather her own rage in the face of *anticipated criticism*. The irrational anger itself was robbing her of energy and self-esteem; the rage inside evoked irrational suspicion and distrust. In expressing and examining her rage, she became aware of shame, hurt, feelings of being useless, and her obsessive screaming and yelling. She saw other qualities: feeling stifled; feeling frustrated, helpless, misunderstood, rejected; fighting to catch her breath; being aware of a constriction of her entire body, particularly in her throat, a dryness, a terrifying feeling that at any moment her heart would stop and she would be unable to breathe. Looking again at her raging response to significant others' behavior, she became aware of thoughts of betrayal, revenge, memories of being unjustly punished, of being unfairly attacked, of family forces of evil at work against her, and feelings of being small and squeezed in by others. The horizons of her experience of rage deepened and expanded each time she focused on them. New horizons opened. Rage not only colored but, to a large degree, determined her most critical moments of pain and sorrow in everyday living.

The person in therapy must choose what goes into the bracket for search, expression, illumination, and resolution. She or he must be free to make shifts, but once an issue becomes the dominant one, the therapist remains with that focus, employing statements and questions that will encourage fuller descriptions and elucidations of the problem.

In summary, Bracketing involves a central issue or problem and grows out of an encompassing determination to let the problem manifest itself in all its connections to self and

others. The bracketed phenomenon remains the focus until
there is a sense of closure that may satisfy the purpose of the
therapy or lead to a shift to another problem that has become
paramount in the consciousness of the person in therapy.

## Horizonalization

Once within the bracket, every expression of the person in
therapy, every point on the horizon of the person's world,
is accepted as having equal validity and value. Horizonalization means that therapist and person in therapy receive
whatever emerges as the focus of the problem. The therapist
is committed to making no judgments regarding the value
of the material presented. Initially, every statement is horizonal and treated with equal care and respect. Horizonalization is a wonderful antidote to selective listening, to the
biased mind that establishes a hierarchy of what matters, the
listening that judges, for example, that sexual references are
more revealing than anything else. In horizonalization, every
statement is equally important. The challenge is to let everything that appears in consciousness, relevant to the issue,
stand out in its own way, accepting all of it, receiving all of
it, valuing all of it. During this phase of phenomenological
psychotherapy, the therapist encourages the person in
therapy to tell the whole story, as it emerges. Everything is
received without evaluation, diagnosis, or prognosis. Each
statement has a respected place in efforts to understand.
Throughout, the therapist guides the person in therapy toward description and explication of the horizons of his or
her experience.

When the person in therapy has difficulty in beginning,
the therapist might suggest an activity for relaxation and say,
"Let yourself be open to anything that appears in your conscious awareness when you consider this issue; let the highlights appear that are connected with your concern, from
your earliest memories to the present; let them enter your

consciousness and just describe them as they appear to you, what you feel and think as you consider this issue, the scenes that awaken in you, the places, incidents, and people that stand out. This will help us to understand more fully your distressing experiences and how they came to be."

The task of the therapist is to obtain descriptions of horizonal experiences, the angles, perspectives, feelings, people, and views connected with the bracketed issue or problem. By considering every offering an important dimension of the person's world, the therapist is accepting the person's choices regarding what to articulate, what to express, what to deepen and expand. The therapist is encouraging the unfolding of meanings that underlie happenings in the person's internal and external life. Such a process in its unfolding involves a continual creation of one's self "by each separate act, each free choice in daily living" (Sartre 1963, p. 23).

Horizonalization involves patience and gradualness, a waiting stance that supports whatever is to be by letting *whatever is* exhaust itself in its own time and space. The horizonalization process can be completed in a fifty-minute hour or over several weeks, but as long as the person in therapy stays within the bracketed phenomenon, the therapist does not interrupt the process or abort it but rather remains there in that other person's bracketed world, remains there until the person in therapy is ready to bring the horizons of her or his world into thematic concentration. What is in this person's world is moved by intentional sources of energy and life that will determine the nature and meaning of perception, feeling, hoping, willing, judging, and other acts of consciousness. Whether the communications are "vital" or "inconsequential" is not for the therapist to assess. The appearance is all that matters and the unfolding of what appears in consciousness in varying perspectives and expressions. The very structure of consciousness directs people to the entities, events, and situations that have meaning in a particular time and space.

As phenomenological therapists, our task is to encourage and support intentional experience, that which appears and is expressed. In that way, in our acceptance and affirmation, we enable an unfolding process that ultimately leads to core knowledge of what is permeating and essential in the person's self and world. Through the horizonalization process, we are able to make direct contact with original data, with original material that emerges concretely in the conscious awarenesses of the experiencing person. Otherwise, as Sartre (1963) explains, "we can no longer find 'the one' to whom that experience has happened; either in looking for the person, we encounter a useless metaphysical substance—or else the being whom we seek vanishes in a dust of phenomena bound together by external connections" (pp. 51–52). Support of what is there in a person's conscious experiences enables what is there to unfold with ever-increasing meaning; it enables individuals to disclose and reveal themselves and to become more and more who they really are, thus removing distortions of everyday living and reaching toward authenticity and essence. What is within the consciousness of the person in therapy is self-knowledge and self-evidence, basic fundamental elements of the person's life-world.

## Delimiting Meanings and Explicating Themes

Once the therapist obtains a complete description of the issue or problem that has been bracketed, phenomenological psychotherapy moves toward a delimiting of core meanings and joining them into encompassing themes.

In delimiting, the therapist looks for meanings, qualities, and themes that characterize and permeate the experience. In selecting themes for further study, for example, of the bracketed rage described earlier, the person in therapy emphasized feelings of uselessness and helplessness and feelings of being stifled, rejected, and shamed. These were linked to the broad theme "Inferiority and Self-Doubt." In the therapy, this theme was explored in depth. It awakened childhood memories, and as the experience of rage was further explored, the theme took on different meanings. Adolescent experiences of inadequacy were examined, situations in which the self was denied, blocked, and restrained, and in which the self was dominated by others. Stella began to consider ways of creating a genuine self that would have its own character, strength, and confidence. She found within herself ways that capitalized on resources rather than being tied to shortcomings and deficiencies. She began to understand self-evidence as a basis for knowledge and action and to depend on her own assessments rather than the evaluations of others.

In Pat's therapy with Sally, the horizonalization process included Sally's description of thoughts and feelings that she experienced during and following the death of her grandfather, her feelings of being abandoned by her father, and her alienation from her mother. She conveyed to Pat a sense that there was no one in her world, absolutely no one who loved her or cared what happened to her. In delimiting Sally's horizons of abandonment, the theme of loneliness dominated, the feeling of being entirely alone in the world became the central concern. Sally described her loneliness as feeling "like a broken bird in a cage, hurt and defenseless, empty, filled with pain, left out." The only person who she felt ever loved her had died, and, with his death, hope and meaning had also come to an end.

In the delimiting process, persons in therapy select core themes, focus their attention on them and explicate their nature and meaning. The process itself contributes to the lifting out of feelings and thoughts that have interfered with and blocked the growth process. Removal of these restraints is achieved by explicating themes that have predisposed the person to hold onto a frozen and destructive past, a narrowing of the world and a constriction of the self. The process is facilitated by the person's descriptive accounts of personal and interpersonal tensions, frustrations, conflicts, and alienations from self, body, and world. The descriptive method itself facilitates explication of meanings connected with the bracketed phenomenon. Various textural perspectives are offered; descriptions of the way things appear in situations of fear, stress, upheaval or danger are presented. The laying hold of these, looking at them again and again, brings them into closer view, and, as they are experienced, the anxiety of the person in therapy is reduced. Much of the pain evoked by destructive events is dissipated during the thematic description and explication. The therapist enters into each of these moments, helps keep them alive, raises questions that will extend awareness and understanding, listens for references to time, space, self, other, causality, and bodily concerns, and points to the conditions through which the issue came to have such power in the person's life.

Smith (1979), in discussing the descriptive method, states:

> [T]hrough the descriptive process we try to elucidate "that which" appears and "the how" of its appearing. In the realm of human experiencing and behavior, as in the therapeutic situation, we are faced with matrices of meaning, configurations of intentionalities. The first mode of their appearing is not usually fully and clearly present to us. . . . [T]he descriptive procedure seeks to explicate, to unfold what is appearing and what we are present to. . . . To describe is to draw out what is given." [p. 42]

## Comprehensive Textural Description

In the next phase of phenomenological psychotherapy the aim is to bring together the various textural qualities of an experience into a unified whole, integrating the core themes and their textural qualities into a descriptive portrait of the person, into what is central in her or his intentional experiences; the phenomena that appear in consciousness and affect the person's sense of self, time, space, relations with others, bodily feelings and states, and the connections between self and experience. These are woven together in one of several ways. The person in therapy might, as a home assignment, be asked to write a textural description of the bracketed phenomenon, based on an integration of the meanings and themes; or the therapist might write the description, or both therapist and person in therapy might separately construct a textural description.

Up to this point in therapy, segments, components, and themes have been central; the challenge now is to construct a picture of the experience as a whole. This means organizing what matters in the person's world related to the problem into a unity of interconnecting components or parts. This integration facilitates movement toward the next major phase of phenomenological psychotherapy, Imaginative Variation.

Following the development of the textural description, therapist and person in therapy examine it together. The person in therapy makes whatever corrections are needed, pauses to reflect on aspects of the description, particularly those that awaken further associations and recollections and those related to present realities and future possibilities. A final textural description is constructed. It becomes available for the structural exploration, the search to discover how the experience of the bracketed phenomenon is precipitated, what conditions exist that bring the problem or issue into consciousness and make it a compelling and powerful focus of the person's life.

## Illustrations of Phenomenological Reduction

Stella's textural description was based on two themes that had been the focus of her therapy—life within herself and life within her family. What appeared and lingered was a sense of being continually isolated, frightened, alone with

doubts and uncertainties, and a sense of defeat and failure
as a person and as a mother and wife. This was in contrast
with how her world might change and become more fulfilling, caring, and happy. The first descriptive portrait captured
what manifested itself in a world of suffering and misery,
the second in a world of joy and fulfillment.

## A World of Misery

I am always upset, tight, feel powerless. I get confused about
things and don't know what to do. I feel like giving up. I think
about Vietnam where I was born, the destruction and death;
my mother and father; my brothers and sisters so far away. I
feel desolate and alone. My kids suffer; they are out of control, like jackrabbits. No one listens to me. I get raging mad,
like a fierce dog, barking shrilly but that doesn't help. I get
so mad at times I feel like killing someone, like a violent man
but I know I won't do anything like that. I know I can't. My
sleep is restless. I'm all tangled up. In my sleep, I shout and
get angry and more angry, tighten up like a knot. I want to
scream like a howling wolf at the edge of a cliff. No one will
listen; no one will hear. I want to leave, run far away but I
know clearly that that will not get me where I want to go.

## A World of Happiness

I see how my communications can be improved, how I can
express my feelings directly, not by screaming, but by sitting
with John or the kids and saying what it is like for me. I see
how by meeting in this way we can really get along, come to
know one another, and share and love one another. The kids
are growing up. They are learning to listen and seeing that
their parents listen to them. There is less fighting when we
are together in these ways. The conflicts that occur are
handled. The kids have friends and play well with them. I
see myself feeling relaxed and happy. I enjoy my life. I feel
calm when talking and know that my family is listening to
me and to one another.

In the textural description, the therapist searches for clues pointing to meanings that will further elucidate and guide the life of the person in therapy toward well-being and growth. In the preceding descriptions, communication is a central theme; when one is not listened to, not heard, one is driven to seek destructive outlets to express one's feelings. When one is heard, one awakens to feelings of presence, love, and happiness.

In the Imaginative Variation, Stella discovered that effective and caring communication is the key to happiness. She envisioned a way to affirm herself and establish a positive family identity.

## Higher- and Lower-Order Hallucinations

Van Dusen (1973) employed a phenomenological psychotherapy in his studies of hallucinations of hospitalized people. He developed a relationship with them and also with the fantasized voices they were seeing and hearing. He held lengthy dialogues with the hallucinations, recording his own questions and their answers. Van Dusen states, "My method is that of phenomenology. My only purpose was to come to as accurate description as possible of the patient's experience" (p. 121). He learned that there are lower-order and higher-order hallucinations and that the function of those in the lower order is to reveal the person's weaknesses. They are irreligious or antireligious (p. 123). In contrast, the higher-order hallucinations are symbolic, religious, supportive, genuinely instructive, and communicate directly (p. 125).

## The Experience of Addiction

Another example of textural description involved a young man suffering from a long-term drug addiction. Robert, a doctoral intern, brought his presuppositions regarding addiction into his work as a drug counselor. He decided to approach the person in therapy, Don, in a phenomenological way. He first engaged in a process of Epochē, setting aside previous perceptions and attitudes regarding the drug experience. He entered the session with an open attitude. He invited Don, following Initial Engagement, to describe his drug experience. Throughout, Robert was aware of setting aside biases and listening actively to receive what was offered and to understand what was given. Here is an excerpt from Don's textural description:

> It's like a kind of rush . . . like a chill running down your back. It's like someone poured cold water on you. There's a scared feeling like, "What am I gonna do now." My nerves are instantly shot! I gotta get some dope—I gotta do something. And then it's like I'll never make it! When you're at the dope house you get real impatient waiting for the dope man. . . . You keep hearing things and say, "Is that him—he's late!" You feel like you'll never make it. You get real agitated and jumpy and want to bite off all your fingernails. And there's gagging and dry-heaving and you really get the sweats. Sometimes I feel like I'm just gonna explode. I get desperate, and it's completely uncontrollable.

## Concluding Comments

Another value of textural descriptions relates to the process of writing. The construction of a textural description itself is a creative act, an opportunity to develop in written form what has manifested itself, an opportunity to see just what is central, just what matters. To write texturally is a way of being and living, of bringing what matters to conscious awareness, viewing the core qualities and themes of one's experience and seeing what they mean. Writing is a way of envisioning what is and what might be. The writing offers a resource for further engagement and impact, perhaps an inspiration to continue to work toward growing as a self, extending possibilities and meanings, being committed to resolution of an issue, and discovering ways of being; for example, developing projects that will contribute to affirmation and valuing of one's self, and moving toward people who are supportive and caring and away from people who demean and criticize.

## IMAGINATIVE VARIATION

The next major process of phenomenological psychotherapy is Imaginative Variation. The primary emphasis during this phase is that of looking at possibilities, views, perspectives, and directions that might offer new frames of reference, and new meanings, for altering one's life and enhancing one's sense of self, heightening body awarenesses, enriching one's relationships with others, and developing new life and work projects. Included in the unfolding of this process of phenomenological psychotherapy are Free Fantasy and Perspectival Variation, Deriving Structural Themes, and Developing a Comprehensive Structural Description.

### Free Fantasy and Perspectival Variation

During this process the therapist encourages the person in therapy to fantasize freely the possible meanings connected with the bracketed phenomenon. Attention is given to how different members of a family and other significant persons view the person in therapy, especially with reference to the bracketed phenomenon. In this process, images, visions, and scenes are created, and the issue is viewed from many vantage points. Time and space are altered by varying perspectives and possible outcomes. The possible in phenomenological psychotherapy is regarded as a dimension of what is true, a potential reality that first comes into existence in imagination or in fantasy.

What is in imagination has connections with real knowledge and experience. Thus imagination is a significant dimension of psychotherapy and facilitates an unfolding reality. What I believe or imagine or fantasize is something coming into existence. I can shift from a miserable world to a joyous one to some degree, if I can envision how joy might enter my world. The imagining of something, in its voices and sounds, in its colors and visions, is real. In its language and meanings it contains not only the possible but something real on the way. When I pursue an imaginary path in perception, feeling or judgment, I am already moving toward its creation. My perception or feeling or judgment is directed toward something real, whether it actually exists at the moment or not. In phenomenological therapy the free-fantasizing, and varying of perspectives, is based on the knowledge and experience of the person in therapy and the therapist. The therapist guides the imaginative journey on the basis of clues drawn from the comprehensive textural description. The textural description offers possible meanings relevant to universal structures—time, space, relation to self and others, bodily concerns, causality, and movement. These are connected with inner consciousness of past, present, and future life.

Truth includes the possible, the meanings that grow out of illuminations of what might be. In this sense, truth is both existent and imaginary. Combining the existent and the imaginary offers a more complete picture of "what is" and "what is becoming" in the world of the person in therapy. This later focus is a central emphasis of Free Fantasy and Perspectival Variation in phenomenological psychotherapy. Imagined scenes suggest possibilities that may become realities in the dramas of living.

Clues based on what is possible are utilized in expanding what is known. The mystery of the unknown and movement toward its illumination are inherent in the imaginative wanderings of the person in therapy. These wanderings may be approached through fantasy trips or guided imagery, through exploration of polarities, and through descriptions of how one's mother, father, husband, or children view the person in therapy. This process points to how things might be, what conditions precipitate the experience of the phenomenon, what constructions are made to turn the possible toward the real.

## Illustration: Free-Fantasy Variation

In an example of phenomenological psychotherapy, June, the therapist, created the Free-Fantasy/Perspectival Variation of a bracketed phenomenon and shared it with Mary, the person in therapy. The question of focus was "Shall I divorce my husband?" The following variations of meaning were constructed.

### The Therapist's View

"I'm free" filled me with a sense of relief and excitement. I recalled the countless times that Mary had considered that her despair was being reinforced daily by living in a toxic situation; that if she chose to stay with an unhappy marriage, she needed to do so out of a sense of choice rather than fear of alternatives. My excitement came from the hope that now her life and our therapy sessions might move in a more positive and productive direction. I believed that she had finally reached a turning point. I saw her as a free, responsible and happy person.

*How her husband might view divorce*: He might be filled with anger that she, who has been so difficult to live with for so many years, was now going to leave him. On the other hand, he might be relieved that she was making the move, so that he did not have to do so himself. It is possible that his self-esteem would be hurt, since he might interpret this as a rejection of him. He might feel anger toward me as her therapist, since it was through her therapy that she decided to make this break.

*How her daughter, age 18, might view the divorce*: She would probably understand her mother's need to live a better life, since the two of them have been rather open with each other. She might experience it as permission to make choices that felt right in her own life. She might decide to move out with her mother, to alleviate the conflict she has had with her father. She also might feel abandoned, or angry that she feels she has to choose between living with her father or mother.

*Viewpoint of her best friend* (also a married woman): She would be glad if Mary had an apartment alone where they could share their friendship. She might feel threatened that Mary would want her to leave her family, too. She would be pleased at the shift from helplessness to power in her friend. She would see me as a successful therapist in having helped Mary move to this point.

From a structural examination of the perspectival variations, Mary experienced a definite shift in the realization of freedom of choice and in imagining how her new life might be as a single adult. Consideration of the different perspectives enabled Mary to view the divorce as a necessary action and provided her with an encouragement to take the decisive step and move into an apartment of her own.

As in all the phases of phenomenological psychotherapy, the Free-Fantasy/Perspectival Variation process is presented to the person in therapy as a way to view underlying meanings. The therapist's statements and questions encourage descriptive expressions and guide the direction of therapy toward new experiences, toward an understanding of the essences of the bracketed phenomenon, texturally and structurally.

In this process, the therapist draws out free and open possibilities and moves toward the explication of structural themes—descriptions of feelings, perceptions, judgments, and other conscious experiences; projected possibilities and meanings in relation to self, others and world. As the process unfolds, certain meanings will recur, certain possibilities will repeat themselves, certain dimensions and constituents of the projected will stand out as unvarying. These open

the way to the development of core themes and their explication, the next phase of phenomenological psychotherapy.

## Invariant Themes

Careful, disciplined listening throughout the process of
qualitative interviewing enables the therapist, who is utilizing phenomenological psychotherapy, to derive from Free
Fantasy and Perspectival Variation, the structural themes
that stand out, the invariant themes that reveal *how* it is that
the person in therapy is predisposed to feeling, seeing, perceiving, judging, being with oneself and others, in just the
ways that the person has described. The core or dominant
themes are chosen for concentrated focus and explication.
The interviewing process encourages articulation of descriptive qualities of these themes. Therapist and person in therapy
agree on the selected themes that are central in understanding
how the person views life and how these views motivate and
precipitate certain situations, events, issues, and problems.
A continuing, close connection exists between conscious,
noetic experiences (*how* it is that the person views things in
the way they are viewed) and the noematic qualities that are
awakened (*what* the person feels, thinks, perceives, intuits,
senses, judges, recalls).

In phenomenological therapy with Marion, Delores (a
doctoral psychotherapy intern with sixteen years' practice
as a psychiatric social worker) focused on a bracketed issue
that Joyce herself had indicated was her major concern.
Together they formulated the problem "Something is missing inside me. There is something wrong with me. I am lack-
ing something essential to my living." Marion added, "The
times when I am most aware that something is missing is
when I am confused, not knowing what to do, feeling lost.
Then my tears begin to flow and I feel deeply saddened."

For the next seven interviews, the focus of the therapy was
the bracketed "something is missing in me":

1. Memories of elementary school in which she was vividly aware of not sharing anything personal, not disclosing her feelings, not trusting anyone

2. Recollection of a junior high incident in which she was put in charge of her class while the teacher left the room. She recalled her inability to effect order, the yelling and running and throwing of things, and finally her total collapse, her sense of failure, and uncontrollable weeping

3. Fear of expressing herself publicly, illustrated in her description of an event in which she finally publicly read a brief statement and then depreciated her effort

4. Reference to a recent morning family experience in which everything she did turned to disaster—burning toast, dropping bacon on the floor, not letting the dog out in time

5. Describing a situation in which a colleague was being praised by her supervisor in Marion's presence. Marion perceived this to mean that the supervisor considered her an incompetent employee. She disclosed a series of incidents in which she had failed to respond sensitively to injury or accident of others, including her children. She described her feeling of anger in these situations and concluded that there was something wrong with her

6. Describing a family scene in which she criticized her mother for sloppy housekeeping, for serving Marion and her husband "crummy leftovers." In the process of revealing these feelings, she berated her behavior as an act of cruelty toward her mother. "I feel that I am not a Christian; I am a bad person, attacking her when I should be honoring her as my mother." (Marion wept silently for the remaining forty-five minutes of this session).

Marion also disclosed incidents with men who tried to seduce her, including her husband's associates. She condemned herself, not them, and repeated that something must be wrong with her, because they interpreted her behavior as sexual invitations.

Each of these horizons was fully explored. The themes that stood out as central in what was missing in Marion's life were: making destructive comparisons with others, feeling incompetent, being out of control, and unfairly evaluating significant people in her life. Each of these constituents of the "something missing" contributed to her feeling that something was wrong with her, that she was a misfit and a failure. Within each of the horizons was a counter force, a movement toward honesty, integrity, and genuine concern for others. Two invariant themes were derived as the structural horizons of Marion's world: Discovering Self-Confidence and Being in Control. When these were evoked as guiding forces in her life, Marion felt good, honest, clear, strong; she related to others with integrity and communicated directly; she presented herself openly and was positively received. When these qualities were absent, she felt confused, weak, inadequate, bad. At such times, she experienced her life as painful, heavy, a disaster.

Marion and Delores agreed that the next focus of their therapy would be the full explication of the invariant themes: Being in Control and Discovering Self-Confidence. The challenge would be to construct imaginative activities and establish resources for carrying them out, in such a way that these values would emerge as central in her relations with others.

## SYNTHESIS AND PLAN OF ACTION

The final phase of phenomenological psychotherapy requires that therapist and person in therapy integrate the textural and structural descriptions into a comprehensive portrayal of the essences of the bracketed phenomenon. The aim is to bring together the *what* of the person's experience and the *how* in such a way that its nature and meanings are embraced. This includes seeking a resolution through an understanding and discovery of what is required to create new perceptions and feelings and to express them in everyday living. The synthesis is not a summary but an intuitive, imaginative creation of the core meanings and essences of the phenomenon that has been the focal point of therapy.

## The Experience of Depression

Warren entered my office slowly, very slowly. I moved bodily with him, while standing still. With each of his steps, there was a marked heaviness. He appeared to be carrying a weighty burden. For a few moments, we sat in silence. His head was bowed and he said, almost in a whisper, "During the last few days I have been almost continually depressed." I suggested that he remain quiet and allow himself just to be with whatever awakened in him. He did not respond verbally, but something in his facial expression told me that he welcomed this opportunity, not to feel pressed to say or do anything at all. I, too, found the moment of silence refreshing, viewed it as an opportunity to clear my own mind from thoughts connected with an extremely busy morning, during which I had not had time to open myself fully and be ready for this meeting with Warren. I closed my eyes, as Warren did, breathed deeply and was aware of becoming fully present with him, ready to receive whatever he offered. In this peaceful and relaxed state, I looked toward Warren, continued to sit with him in silence, as he struggled to come to terms with his depression.

He looked up, our eyes met. I felt the sadness grow between us. Then, I encouraged him to put into words what he was painfully experiencing inwardly.

C:  Warren, I would like you to describe what you've been thinking and feeling regarding your depression, what is its nature, what is the depression directed toward. (A brief silence followed.)

W: I have become extremely discouraged about my future. I had anticipated that by this time I would have developed an adequate private practice and would have begun to make preparations to resign as a priest, to leave my parish. I look ahead and wonder why I am unable to attract more clients; I seem to be stuck with a minimal number, barely ten meetings a week. And now in the last few days some of my cases are terminating. I have no idea where new people will come from. I am no more secure in my efforts to attain financial stability than I was six months ago. The unknown and unpredictable have become my enemy. I feel extremely frustrated by the ambiguity of my whole world. Sometimes I am overwhelmed with the sense that nothing is settled in my life, nothing at all.

C: Time has become a burden to you, closing in on you, in a sense imprisoning you, and keeping you from moving ahead.

W: Yes, that's true. The future right now is closing in on me, giving me the feeling that my life is slipping away. But this is only part of my worry. I believe that my depression is also connected with my life as a priest. The parishioners that I am most involved with, that I have come to know intimately, are getting older and I feel deeply saddened, witnessing their loss of energy and vitality, and living with their illnesses. Just last week another of my parish friends died and one entered a nursing home, disabled by a major stroke. Each week I face similar painful endings. I want to move on; I am ready to move on. Yet I wonder how it will be when I actually leave. My life as a priest still has some hold on me, especially the people. Will they be angry with me? Will they feel like I have abandoned them? I believe that the bishop will understand and support my decision to seek a new profession. He won't be happy but he will accept it. Time is a factor; it does press me.

W:  Next year begins the 100th birthday of my parish. I will not leave until the year ends but that will be the right time. The way in which I'm progressing in my work as a psychotherapist provides no encouragement. When the 100th year events and celebrations are over, I'll be transferred (the bishop informed me of this a few weeks ago) to another parish. I do not want to begin the process all over again. I am ready to move on, ready to begin a secular life. I have a great deal I can bring to helping people grow. I can serve more freely and without all the political and social pressures that fall on me as a parish priest.

C:  Your depression is connected with a sense of urgency to move on with life, with daily reminders of life diminishing, with being surrounded with aging people and with death and dying. Time is pushing you to take a decisive step but you are afraid that you will not be able to establish yourself and attain financial security. You've already built into your consciousness a future of full practice as a psychologist and you are already viewing the priesthood as part of the past. Yet, neither this future nor the past is a completed process; movement appears to be denied you, and you are fixed or frozen in a present that is not at all satisfying.

W:  I do not always feel this kind of depression. I am in it now because my involvement with people means terminating both in the parish and the clinic. So perhaps I am in the process of dealing with dying, and with death, but it is not so much death but the unknown that is paralyzing me. I don't know where I'm going, for sure, either in a career as a psychologist or in my vows as a priest. (Brief pause)

Another component of my life is just now coming into my awareness, also connected to my depression. I am in the process of informing my family that I will be resigning as a priest. They have viewed me as a priest now for over twenty-five years. Something is dying there too, the way we've met and talked, their placing onto me certain sacred values and confidences. I do not know what they will think when I resign, what they will feel. I can feel the sadness just now as I imagine my talks with them, and their sadness too, though I believe they will accept my decision.

A silence followed. Warren seemed very absorbed in these latest disclosures. He had completed the horizonalization process of phenomenological psychotherapy. As I understood the process, the highlights of his experience of depression were as follows:

*The Challenge of Change*—the frustrations and stresses, the problems and challenges in movement toward leaving the priesthood and becoming a fully practicing psychologist

*Uncertainty*—self-doubt in facing a shaky future and in coming to terms with financial insecurity

*Dying and Death*—the ending of a way of life as a parish priest and with his family, along with the aging of his parishioners and recent deaths of his church friends, as well as his own aging and his sense of urgency to be successful in a new profession

*The Unknown*—the anxiety of not having sufficient evidence that he could succeed as a psychotherapist, not being sure of how his parishioners would respond, and not knowing how his brothers and sisters would deal with his resignation as a priest. The feelings permeating the horizons of his depression were loneliness, fear, sadness, pain, the agony of time, discouragement, frustration, darkness, being burdened and weighted down by the struggle, the slowness and uncertainty of the future. Something within himself is preventing or interfering with his progress and with the development of his confidence in the future.

I shared this textural description with Warren and suggested that the themes that encompassed his depression were Change, Uncertainty, Death and Dying, and the Unknown. He agreed that these were present and added two other themes: Taking a Stand and Being True to Himself. He viewed these as components of his life that were being frustrated and that were contributing to his depression. Yet, he assured me that he already had begun taking a stand with his family and that he was certain that he would take a stand with the church officials, to move on. He affirmed that being true to himself required that he resign as a priest, whatever the consequences.

I asked him whether one of these themes encompassed all of the others, essential to an understanding of them. His response was immediate.

Mystery runs through all of them. When I remind myself of this I immediately feel an uplift. I am feeling it right now. The depression has lifted. Mystery helps me have faith that the change will occur, that my practice will increase, that I will resign as a priest and this will be accepted, that my family will also be accepting and support a direction that will contribute to my happiness, and that I will create a good life with others. Mystery is the key; faith in its powers to reveal, to discover; faith that something will emerge that will bring me into touch with what is needed to achieve financial security, whether private practice or paid employment as a psychotherapist. This is what has been missing lately—my recognition of mystery, my willingness to surrender to mystery. Mystery has always had that power to allow me to deal with change, uncertainty, death and dying, and an unknown future.

With this revelation, my session with Warren ended. Clearly he was a different person; his movements had speeded up; his facial expressions were alive; his energy was visibly heightened. He embraced me warmly and departed.

Warren, in this session, had participated in the Epochē process (as I had), clearing an inward space, opening himself to letting whatever became manifest in his awareness, to appear, linger, and endure, reflected in his descriptions of the various phenomena that emerged. He had described the horizons of his world of depression. He had reduced them to six basic themes: the Challenge of Change, Uncertainty, the Unknown, Death and Dying, Taking a Stand, and Being True to Himself. He had integrated these into one central theme: Mystery. Finally, he had considered many possible meanings of mystery and how they related to his past, present, and future life.

The process itself of explicating and describing the experiences of depression, in the presence of an accepting, affirming, and caring person, lifted the depression out of its frozen space and time and enabled Warren to move on with new spirit, energy, and optimism.

## The Experience of Rage

In his therapy with Joe, David had prepared himself to be receptive and open. He set aside his biases regarding rage and theories to account for it. He refrained from interpreting Joe's behavior from an analytic perspective or to impose ideas that he had constructed from work with other "hostile" people.

Joe was a large man who had difficulty controlling his anger, which sometimes reached raging proportions, particularly when his wife argued with him or disagreed with him. At such times, he released his rage by punching holes into various walls of his home, and as segments of his home fell apart, so did his marriage. When David encouraged him to describe the rage, Joe referred to extreme tensing and straining of muscles, violent breathing, shrieking sounds that came from his body, grotesque changes in his facial appearance, flailing of his arms, and agitated movements of his entire body. While describing his rage, he pounded on David's desk, emphasizing his torment and his need to release the wild animals inside. When Joe had enumerated and described completely the series of battles with his wife and his inability to control his rages, David asked him to consider the opposite kind of experience, event, or situation in which he was totally at peace with his world. Joe responded immediately, referring to his hobby of building model ships.

As he spoke, the picture was forming of a relationship in which there was concern for detail, patience, and caring and time for building, noticing, savoring, and being with his creation. He also described his frustration and irritation in the process of construction, but he had never destroyed what was taking shape. He would inevitably see another way of proceeding. The themes reflected in this situation were carefulness, timelessness, gentleness, and love. He said he would never destroy something he worked so hard to create. David reminded him that he had also worked hard on developing a marriage over a ten-year period. David asked him whether he could take the same kind of caring, involvement, and patience into his relationship with his wife. After all, when his ship did not agree with his way of working with it, he found a constructive, alternative path. Could he not also find a positive option for relating to his wife when she disagreed with him? Joe smiled; he saw the metaphoric connections and resolved that in the intervening week he would look upon building a marriage in the way that he viewed building a ship and keep in mind the importance of patience, commitment, and regard for the other.

David had utilized phenomenological therapy in a flexible way, not in the regular sequence of processes and methods but nonetheless effectively. Of particular importance was Epochē, which he employed several times during the interview ("I had to bite my tongue and back off every time I had an urge to interpret his hostility, dependency, and alcoholism"); Focusing ("What mattered was remaining entirely with his directions and themes, concentrating on his view of things"); and Imaginative Variation ("We really worked hard on viewing the marriage as a metaphor for ship building"). In substance, David did not fit Joe into the phenomenological model. He found strategies for improving and fitting the model into Joe's way of explicating his problem. Throughout, David encouraged description, but he also accepted Joe's explanations and recounting of events. The model itself facilitated openness and flexibility regarding whatever appeared in Joe's consciousness. David varied the sequence and emphasis but remained attuned throughout to Joe's world and Joe's approach to relationships, while also guiding Joe through the phenomenological processes of Epochē, Focusing, and Imaginative Variation.

## Conflict in Relation to One's Father

The following example is a verbatim presentation of the phenomenological psychotherapy process, utilizing Epochē, Phenomenological Reduction, and the first phase of Imaginative Variation. Both Walter, the person in therapy, and his therapist closed the meeting with an understanding of the essences of the experience, and a beginning plan for carrying forward the insights derived. The session began with a brief meditation activity.

*Epochē*

T: Close your eyes, breathe deeply, and clear your mind completely. I know from the way you rushed in here that this has been a busy morning for you; it has for me too. Let's take a little time to relax, clear our minds, and be here together. (four minutes of silent meditation)

*Initial Engagement*

T: Is there something now in central focus that comes into your awareness, something that opens freshly?

W: As I thought about this meeting I found myself going back to this issue that is unresolved—my relationship with my father and his experience in Nazi Germany. It has had a great impact on my life.

T: Just let yourself speak spontaneously, unreflectively, whatever enters your mind.

W: I'll start where I am. The whole thing came into focus for me because I met recently with a close friend whose father is a refugee from a Nazi concentration camp. For several years we've met and talked about the impact of the holocaust on our families. She has wanted me to meet her father who is very ill at this point. I said, "Why don't we go see him now." So we went to the nursing home where he resides and spent a couple of hours there. It was a very, very intense and sad experience. I entered into his sparse world. He had a tremendous amount of pain and I found myself in tears. I just wanted to be there for him.

It seems like that visit connects me to those occasions where my father and I have had intense battles.

T: Your meeting at the nursing home connects you painfully with the struggles and conflicts that you have had with your father. I am not understanding the connection.

W: Well, this man has had a major stroke, and he does not communicate; he says very, very little and that, all my life, has been my struggle with my father—to get him to communicate with me. At times, I've wanted him to face what was underlying his conflict with me; I wanted him to talk with me about what he was thinking and feeling, and he always has refused. He and I have had this series of moments. My most critical moment of my life was when my father walked away from me when I was going away to boarding school as a young child. I had a distinct sense that he had taken me there and said nothing to me, nothing at all; he just walked away. There was not the response from him that I needed. Over the years there were other moments. I can remember once sitting with him in a car. I was on my way back to Israel. He was about to leave me, and I said, "Could you tell me one thing about your childhood?" He was able only to make one sentence and that was a gift that he could manage that. It was always such a struggle between the two of us.

T: You wanted, all those years, just to hear from him, just some word that would tell you what he was thinking and feeling, what was there inside him.

W: Yes, and it was very significant to me when I asked him. Inside himself, as a very important memory of his childhood, was a newspaper clipping of a picture of his mother's store with a caption "Don't buy anything here!" This one sentence brought me so close to him. And then there was a sudden change. I became aware of how many violent battles we have had between us. I remember as a teenager he came into my room, and he was going to physically hit, beat me. I don't think he did. He lunged at me but he was emotionally violent toward me so much of the time. (silence)

T: Rage, rejection was what he expressed.

W: Yes, yet he always wanted me to follow his footsteps, to be in his business. All of that was so intense, then for a while he changed and he became interested in what I wanted to do with my life. At one point, about six years ago we were in Germany together. Again, he started, just out of the blue, to scream and yell at me about being incredibly stupid and everything. I stopped the car and said, "I don't need to put up with this. I'll get my bag and trek home." But, instead, he got out of the car and he started hobbling up the road (he had broken his foot), and I yelled at him, "If you're so stupid that you want to go off and kill yourself, you can." I was absolutely livid, and I was screaming. I mean I was absolutely mad in the fullest sense of that word. "Here", I said, "take your crutch you'll need that." A few minutes later he came back and said, "Well now that we've done that, we can start again." I've always known he wanted to erase everything about me that disturbed him. We were being honest for once. Whatever he had carried inside himself about me, through all the years, was now coming out. It was all coming out, and maybe we could have a fresh start. I was excited at that time, a change was taking place, but I still felt the underlying power trip. I thought, how much better this is, but I didn't totally believe it. After that I wasn't around much. Then, there was his visit here, and throughout that visit I felt very respected by him.

## Bracketing

T: I would like to say that you have offered a very vivid description of the issues connected with your relationship with your father. Is there one event that you would like to focus on, as containing the central issue or problem, in your relationship with your father?

W: Yes, I would like to understand what happens between us that I can come to feel more peaceful about. The last two times we spent any substantial time together, we ended up in enormous conflict.

W: What is the nature and meaning of conflict in my relationship with my father? Is that question one that you would like to focus on in our remaining time?

T: Yes, certainly. Just describe freely what emerges as you consider the question. Take a few moments to return to that situation in which you felt extreme conflict in relation to your father.

*Horizonalization*

W: On that trip last year, there were two occasions in which we faced enormous conflict during a two-week trip. It was so mixed. It was a beautiful trip to go together to a conference on peace, but it was smashed by our fights over his driving. Others refused to ride with him. His night vision, and recognition of colors, was totally impaired. His driving was completely dangerous. My role was to be his eyes, guide him around curves, let him know the color of traffic lights; it was bizarre. I reached a point where I had absolutely no more patience. I was brutal with him. I screamed at him finally, "You can't even read the road sign over there, and you want to drive up a mountain road! I'm not going with you. You'll just kill yourself. I won't allow you to take the car. You're going to have to walk or I'll drive. Or, I'll leave you right here and take the car keys with me." We were there fighting for several hours. Neither of us budging from our position. At one point I said,

"I'm going to leave you here to cool off and I'll be back."

I was away for some time and then walked back to where he was. He threatened to call the police. The only word for the entire fiasco is bizarre, completely bizarre. I had calmed down. I was on the side of insanity where I could function. I was clear about that. I was frightened for him; it would have been easy to walk away from him and let him have the keys, but I felt responsible for him and protective of him.

He finally said, "I can't allow anyone to tell me what to do. That's what the Nazis did. I was forced to do things by their violence." Then I said to him, "I understand that but I don't intend to let you force me to give up the keys and endanger your life." I added, "I'm willing to give you the keys to the car if you'll let me know you've heard what I'm saying and that my judgment has merit." He agreed to that, and after all the hours of fighting, the solution took only five to ten minutes. He drove about 100 yards, stopped the car, handed me the keys, and I drove back to our hotel. He had found such an elegant way to maintain his respect. Needing others can be intensely degrading. In those moments with my father, I saw this whole thing.

Immediately before the violent battle with my father, we had been walking on a mountain road and he actually said to me, "I really enjoyed what you said at the meeting. There was a lot of value to it, and you spoke very sensitively to my colleagues. I really respect what you had to say." I cannot remember any time when he has spoken to me in just that way. I've felt his support before but also his nagging doubts about me. It is hard for me to understand.

The day after the big battle we had another one. He wanted to drive again. I was so angry I had a tem-

per tantrum on the spot, started kicking the dash-
board; I was flailing my arms and legs and yelling
and screaming at him. That is just how I had handled
my frustrations with him as a child when he was
being totally inflexible. (long pause)

## Thematic Explication

T: For me there are certain things that stand out in what
you are sharing with me. I am aware of the very intense relationship that you have with your father, of
underlying feelings of concern and love, of mutual
respect, feelings that are shattered in a situation of
conflict where you hold opposing views. In these
conflicts with your father, there are themes that recur
and in a sense are the conditions that precipitate violent disagreements. One theme is self-esteem, holding onto your perception of things and believing that
your perception is valid. Another theme is integrity.
Each of you is strongly determined to hold onto your
position to take a stand and refuse to be pushed aside.
Threat to the continuing existence of integrity appears
to arouse anger, determination, and, in a sense, a stubborn, unyielding, closed position. A third theme is
strength, maintaining your role as men—a father appearing strong before his son, a son being strong with
his father. Fear of weakness and weakness itself are
regarded as evils.

## Textural Integration

T: Let's focus on the major themes that appear most directly connected with your experience of conflict in
relation to your father: Self-Esteem, Integrity, and
Strength.

W: I see those three as all intimately connected. For me

they are all integrated in the theme of Domination. My reaction to his attempt to control me is to become stubborn, to be furious, to be determined not to give in, to express my rage. The tantrum is how I expressed all of these feelings.

T: Even while you were having your temper tantrum you were maintaining your integrity. You were aware of what you were doing, its effect on your father. There was some strange but definite strength and clarity in it, an act of integrity.

W: Yes, there was integrity in my having the tantrum. I was noncooperative in response to his domination, and I was aware of what I was doing. But I had lost my calm; all the barriers were down.

In the process of this interchange, we became clear that self-esteem, integrity, and not strength, but power were nuclear themes in the experience of conflict in Walter's relationship with his father and that all of these became connected in the theme of domination. Walter continues to explicate this further.

W: I am realizing as we talk that this issue in my life has been so powerful that it has caught up my energy and gotten me involved in what he wanted to do. (long pause)

## Imaginative Variation

T: One question I have is whether you can imagine being in a situation with your father, with a sense of mutuality, of I and Thou, even though it is a situation in which you are in conflict, one where there is strong difference but still where each of you respect the opposite view and where you discover a positive outcome.

W: Well, that's an intriguing idea. I will be seeing my father next month and between now and then I'll be thinking about what you are suggesting, imagining a script where we argue but listen to one another and ultimately come together on an issue.

T: You might find that a positive, growing understanding between you is not only possible but a tangible reality.

W: This time has been really good. Finally, I have an understanding of the nature of conflict in my relationship with my father and how to some degree it is grounded in his life in Nazi Germany. I have not before today gone through the whole thing of what has been involved through the years and what has kept us apart. I know what is essential in being able to carry something through to a point of completion.

## *Follow-up Report*

Following this session, several weeks later, I received a communication from Walter. He had just completed a week-long auto trip with his father, on the West Coast. He had experienced far greater harmony during their travels. With his father's consent, he had done virtually all of the driving. The imagined vision had become reality; the I-Thou "possible life" with his father had become an actual experience. Their communion was now something of definite meaning, one that offered hope for the future.

Before completing this chapter, I contacted Walter and asked whether there was anything he would want to add to my report of our work together using a phenomenological psychotherapy process. I sent him a copy of the report, and he responded with the following *update.*

Looking over the description of the work we did together some eight years ago, I feel an even greater sense of the shift that has occurred in my relationship with my father. While there have, inevitably, been conflicts between us at times, they have never again spiralled out of control, and over the years have become less and less frequent. I view the transcript of my meeting with you as a very accurate presentation of the structure of my relationship with my father and its eventual restructuring to a more positive and hopeful experience.

## Summary: A Model of Phenomenological Psychotherapy

Here I offer an outline that presents the processes and methods that guide the application of phenomenological psychotherapy.

I.  Initial Engagement
    In the Initial Engagement the therapist develops a climate of safety and trust and supports the relaxation, freedom to communicate, and dialogue between the therapist and person in therapy. The therapist enters into the world of the person in therapy and concentrates on his or her internal frame of reference.

II. Epochē
    The therapist abstains from and puts out of action preconceptions, theories, and ideas about the person in therapy, in order to listen with an open mind and hear purely just what is being presented. Prior to the therapy session, the therapist engages in self-dialogue to reduce or eliminate prejudgments and preconceived thoughts and feelings. This process is needed during the actual interview as well when the therapist's thoughts or feelings interfere with listening and accepting the narrative being presented by the person in therapy.

III. Phenomenological Reduction
    This process begins with spontaneous, prereflective communication and gradually moves toward careful

reflections (i.e., thinking, judging, assessing, choosing what is core and what is peripheral).

A. Initial Engagement

During this process, in the first phase of the therapy, the central issue or problem is recognized.

B. Bracketing

The central issue or problem is bracketed—becoming the exclusive center of attention and concentration—in order to search for, express, and illuminate what is essential to resolve the issue or problem.

C. Horizonalization

The therapist receives whatever manifests itself in the consciousness of the person in therapy. The therapist makes no judgments or evaluations of the material presented or its significance. Every statement is received initially as equally important. The therapist encourages the person in therapy to tell the whole story, as it emerges in the person's awareness and understanding. The therapist's acceptance and affirmation facilitate the horizonal process, which leads to core knowledge of what is in the person's self and world.

D. Delimiting and Thematizing

Once the therapist obtains a complete description, from various angles and facets, he or she moves toward the delimiting process—various core constituents of the issue are joined with others in developing encompassing themes. The person in therapy affirms the core themes and focuses attention on them—explicating their nature and meanings. During this process, feelings are lifted out that have blocked the growth process. They are recognized and explicated as a component of focusing on and elucidating the meanings embraced by the core themes.

E. Comprehensive Textural Description

The therapist, with the assistance of the person in

therapy, brings together the various textural constituents into a unified whole, describing the lived experience of the person in his or her world. The therapist
integrates the core themes and their textural descriptions into a unified portrait of the person in therapy.
This process accentuates the phenomena that appear
in the consciousness of the person in therapy and attempts to understand how they affect the person in
his or her everyday world.

IV. Imaginative Variation

The therapist and person in therapy look at possible perspectives and views of the problem, seek new frames of
reference and new meanings to account for the person's
experience—how it is that the person experiences a diminished sense of self, body tensions, and interpersonal
conflicts connected with the problem and its emergence;
what conditions or factors precipitate these qualities and
interfere with resolution of the problem.

A. Free Fantasy

The therapist encourages the person to fantasize
freely on the possible meanings connected with the
bracketed phenomenon. Imaginative scenes are created pertaining to transitional periods of development, guided imagery, fantasy trips, polarities, and
metaphors.

B. Invariant Structural Themes

The structural themes are recognized that reveal how
it is that the person in therapy is predisposed to feeling, seeing, perceiving, and judging in relation to self
and others in just the ways described. Core structural
themes are chosen for concentration and explication.
During the interview, articulation and description of
structural themes are lifted out. These themes are central in understanding how the person views life and
what precipitates crises in self-esteem, communication, and relationships.

V. Synthesis
   During this process, textural and structural descriptions are integrated into a comprehensive description of the essences of the bracketed phenomenon. The synthesis brings together the *what* of the person's experience (textural meanings) and the *how* (structural meanings) in such a way that the phenomenon as a whole is revealed. The synthesis is not a summary, but an intuitive, imaginative creation.

VI. Plan of Action and Follow-Up
   The therapist and person in therapy determine the action required to achieve a resolution of the problem. In a follow-up interview, they assess the effectiveness of the course of action and determine next steps.

## CONCLUDING COMMENTS

The model of phenomenological psychotherapy has been employed by about 150 psychology interns, whom I have supervised, and an equal number of professional psychologists. During applications of phenomenological psychotherapy, interns and psychologists worked with persons faced with a wide range of problems, including drug and alcohol addiction, suicidal tendencies, severe anxiety states, depression, chronic pain, marital crises, and problems of development and transition. The therapy involved children, adolescents, and adults. Without exception, the interns and psychologists reported exciting shifts in the therapy process. They came to value the model as an alternative to other psychotherapy approaches. Bracketing and descriptive methodology brought new life, energy, and spirit into therapy and enabled persons to move forward toward resolution of the problem and action in daily life.

A systematic application of Epoché, Phenomenological Reduction, and Imaginative Variation proved to be an effective process in moving toward synthesis and a plan of action.

Many experiences of employing phenomenological psychotherapy were required to bring about a more or less effortless flow of the process and methodology. Often, it became
necessary for the therapist to engage in Epoché throughout
the process, to continue to insure that the phenomena that
became the focus and their explication were coming from the
person in therapy and not the therapist. Vigilance in this
regard, more and more, facilitated what appeared in consciousness and what supported the person. Bracketing sometimes occurred more than once, when it became clear that
the initially bracketed phenomenon did not linger or was not
a sustaining issue.

In time, the interns and professional psychologists developed their own version of phenomenological psychotherapy,
what fitted their process of working with persons in therapy,
improvising with reference to sequence of the processes, and
varying methods, sometimes weaving texture and structure
throughout the process rather than first constructing a fundamental textural description, followed by a fundamental
structural description, and then integrating the two into an
understanding of the essences of the person's experience
relevant to an issue or problem.

My own application of the model has been a consistently
rewarding experience, bringing a new kind of passionate
involvement into my world and a way of actively participating in the lives of others, a way of witnessing and lifting out
the suffering and its resolution, leading to new relationships,
ventures, and projects. I feel certain that I will continue to
make modifications and refinements of the model but I am
also convinced that as it stands, if offers a valuable resource,
an alternative, in helping persons in therapy move from
despair to hope, from self-denial and self-defeat to self-
affirmation and self-confidence. It offers processes and methods that require effective listening and hearing, seeing things
as they appear and as they are, not judging them, learning
to describe rather than explain or analyze, focusing on a core

problem, lifting out the undisclosed, and pointing the way to conscious involvement and participation.

Phenomenological psychotherapy offers a methodology for creating new ways of looking at life and discovering its nature and meaning, in terms of what is real and what is possible. Over a period of time, persons in therapy themselves can learn to apply the essentials of phenomenological psychotherapy in future crises, in facing issues, problems, or challenges of living. Phenomenological psychotherapy offers a way of interrelating subjective and objective factors and conditions, a way of utilizing description, reflection, and imagination in arriving at an understanding of what is, in seeing the conditions through which what is comes to be, and in utilizing a process that in its very application opens possibilities for awareness, knowledge, and action.

I am convinced, following extensive studies and applications over many years, that the phenomenological approach to human science and to psychotherapy offers an illuminating methodology and processes for discovering knowledge and for resolving the stresses and problems of everyday living, and that it offers a unique resource that opens pathways to creativity, health, and well-being.

# References

Binswanger, L. (1963). *Being in the World*. New York: Basic Books.

Boss, M. (1963). *Psychoanalysis and Daseinsanalysis*, trans. L. Lefebre. New York: Basic Books.

—— (1979). *Existential Foundations in Medicine and Psychology*, trans. S. Conway and A. Cleaves. New York: Jason Aronson.

Buber, M. (1937). *I and Thou*, trans. R. G. Smith. Edinburgh: Clark.

—— (1958). *Hasidism and Modern Man*. New York: Horizon.

Christmas, E. E. (1992). The feeling of being left out (doctoral dissertation, The Union Institute, 1991). *Dissertation Abstracts International* 52 (11B):6079B.

Cohen, J. (1981). *I-Thou relationships with autistic children*. Unpublished doctoral dissertation, Humanistic Psychology Institute, San Francisco.

de Hartman, T. (1972). *Our Life with Mister Gurdjieff*. New York: Penguin.

Dickson, M. (1990). Feeling understood: a heuristic research investigation (doctoral dissertation, The Union Institute, 1991). *Dissertation Abstracts International* 52 (02B):1055B.

Dilthey, W. (1976). *Selected readings*, trans. H. R. Rickman. New York: Cambridge University Press.

Draper, E. D. (1992). Focus. *Parabola* XVII(2):2–3.

Fairfield, R. (1977). *Person-Centered Graduate Education*. Buffalo, NY: Prometheus.

Finch, H. L. (1977). Solipsism—old and new. In *Wittgenstein—The Later Philosophy*, pp. 105–125. Alantic Highlands, NJ: Humanities Press.

Fromm, E. (1976). *To Have or To Be?* New York: Harper & Row.

Gendlin, E. (1972). Therapeutic procedures with schizophrenic patients. In *Theory and Practice of Psychotherapy with Specific Disorders*, ed. M. Hammer. New York: Charles C Thomas.

———— (1978). *Focusing*. New York: Everest House.

Gurdjieff, G. I. (1984). The first initiation. *Parabola* 9(1):6–8.

Hall, E. (1984). *The Dance of Life*. New York: Anchor.

Heidegger, M. (1949). *Existence and Being*. Chicago: Regnery-Gateway.

———— (1962). *Being and Time*, trans. J. Macquarrie and E. Robinson. New York: Harper & Row.

———— (1966). *Disclosure on Thinking*, trans. J. Anderson and H. Freund. New York: Harper & Row.

———— (1968). *What Is Called Thinking*, trans. J. Gray. New York: Harper & Row.

———— (1971). The thinker as poet. In *Poetry, Language, Thought*, trans. A. Hofstadter, pp. 1–14. New York: Harper & Row.

———— (1972). *On Time and Being*, trans. J. Stambaugh. New York: Harper & Row.

———— (1977). Building, dwelling, thinking. In *Basic Writings*, ed. D. Knell. New York: Harper & Row.

Henry, J. (1963). *Culture against Man*. New York: Random House.

Hesse, H. (1951). *Siddhartha*. New York: New Directions.

Imber-Black, E., Roberts, J., and Whiting, R. (1988). *Rituals in Families and Family Therapy*. New York: Norton.

James, W. (1948). *Essays in Pragmatism*. New York: Macmillan.

Jung, C. (1957). *The Undiscovered Self*, trans. R. F. C. Hull. New York: New American Library.

Kazantzakis, N. (1975). *Report to Greco*. New York: Touchstone.

Keen, E. (1975). *A Primer in Phenomenological Psychology*. New York: Holt, Rinehart & Winston.

Klee, J. (1982). *Points of Departure: Aspects of the Tao*. South Bend, IN: And Books.

Lawrence, D. H. (1961). *The Rainbow*. New York: Viking.

Levinson, D. J. (1977). The mid-life transition. *Psychiatry* 40:2.

Lindbergh, A. M. (1955). *Gift from the Sea*. New York: Pantheon.

Lockhart, R. A. (1978). Eros in language, myth, and dream. *Quadrant* II(1):41–68.

Lusseyran, J. (1987). *And There Was Light*. New York: Parabola.

Maslow, A. (1971). *The Farther Reaches of Human Nature*. New York: Viking.

Mathiessen, P. (1978). *The Snow Leopard*. New York: Viking.

McGlashan, A. (1976). *The Savage and Beautiful Country*. New York: Stonehill.

Miller, A. (1987). *All My Sons*. Edgemont, GA: Chelsea House.

Moustakas, C. (1953). *Children in Play Therapy: A Key to Understanding Normal and Disturbed Emotions*. New York: McGraw-Hill.

———— (1956a). *Psychotherapy with Children*. New York: Harper & Row.

————, ed. (1956b). *The Self: Explorations in Personal Growth*. New York: Harper & Row.

———— (1956c). *The Teacher and the Child*. New York: McGraw-Hill.

———— (1961). *Loneliness*. Englewood Cliffs, NJ: Prentice-Hall.

———— (1966a). *The Authentic Teacher*. Cambridge, MA: Doyle.

————, ed. (1966b). *Existential Child Therapy*. New York: Basic Books.

———— (1967). *Creativity and Conformity*. New York: Van Nostrand.

———— (1968). *Individuality and Encounter*. Cambridge, MA: Doyle.

———— (1969). *Personal Growth: The Struggle for Identity and Human Values*. Cambridge, MA: Doyle.

———— (1972a). *Loneliness and Love*. Englewood Cliffs, NJ: Prentice-Hall.

———— (1972b). *Teaching as Learning*. New York: Ballantine.

———— (1974a). *Finding Yourself, Finding Others*. Englewood Cliffs, NJ: Prentice-Hall.

———— (1974b). *Portraits of Loneliness and Love*. Englewood Cliffs, NJ: Prentice-Hall.

———— (1975a). *The Touch of Loneliness*. Englewood Cliffs, NJ: Prentice-Hall.

———— (1975b). *Who Will Listen? Children and Parents in Therapy*. New York: Ballantine.

———— (1977a). *Creative Life.* New York: Van Nostrand.

———— (1977b). *Turning Points.* Englewood Cliffs, NJ: Prentice-Hall.

———— (1981). *Rhythms, Rituals and Relationships.* Detroit: Center for Humanistic Studies.

———— (1987). *Laura.* Unpublished poem, Detroit.

———— (1988). *Phenomenology, Science and Psychotherapy.* Sydney, Nova Scotia: University College of Cape Breton, Family Life Institute.

———— (1990). *Heuristic Research: Design, Methodology and Applications.* Newbury Park, CA: Sage.

———— (1994a). *Phenomenological Research Methods.* Newbury Park, CA: Sage.

———— (1994b). *The silence of being.* Unpublished poem. Detroit.

———— (1994c). *Truth.* Unpublished poem, Detroit.

Moustakas, C., and Berson, M. P. (1956). *The Young Child in School.* New York: Morrow.

Moustakas, C., and Perry, C. (1973). *Learning to Be Free.* Englewood Cliffs, NJ: Prentice-Hall.

Moustakas, K. (1993). Encounters of intimate bonding: an heuristic investigation (doctoral dissertation, The Union Institute, 1992). *Dissertation Abstracts International* 54:504B.

Neruda, P. (1972). *New Poems.* New York; Grove.

Nietzsche, F. (1966). *Thus Spake Zarathustra,* trans. T. Common. New York: Modern Library.

Onda, A. (1972). Satori (enlightenment) of Zen and creativity. In *Abstract Guide of XXth International Congress of Psychology,* p. 588. Tokyo: International Congress of Psychology.

Perry, C. E. (1991). *A heuristic search through self-confrontation.* Unpublished manuscript, Detroit: Center for Humanistic Studies.

Polanyi, M. (1958). *Personal Knowledge.* Chicago: University of Chicago Press.

———— (1964). *Science, Faith, and Society.* Chicago: University of Chicago Press.

———— (1966). *The Tacit Dimension.* New York: Doubleday.

———— (1969). *Knowing and Being.* Chicago: University of Chicago Press.

Rank, O. (1950). *Will Therapy and Truth and Reality,* trans. J. Taft. New York: Knopf.

Rilke, R. M. (1941). *Book of Hours,* trans. B. Deutsch. Norfolk, CT: New Directions.

Roads, M. (1987). *Talking with Nature.* Tiburn, CA: H. J. Kramer.

Rogers, C. (1961). *On Becoming a Person.* Boston: Houghton Mifflin.

——— (1969). *Freedom to Learn.* Columbus, OH: Merrill.

——— (1980). *A Way of Being.* Boston: Houghton Mifflin.

——— (1989). *Carl Rogers: Dialogues,* ed. H. Kirschenbaum and V. L. Henderson. Chapter 4, Paul Tillich, pp. 64–78. Boston: Houghton Mifflin.

Rowe, J. O., Halling, S., Davis, E., et al. (1989). The psychology of forgiving another: a dialogal research approach. In *Existential-Phenomenological Perspectives in Psychology,* ed. R. Valle and S. Halling, pp. 233–244. New York: Plenum.

Rushdie, S. (1992). Our lives teach us who we are. *The Chronicle of Higher Education* XXXVIII (18):B5.

Saint-Exupery, A. (1943). *The Little Prince,* trans. K. Woods. New York: Harcourt, Brace & World.

Salk, J. (1983). *Anatomy of Reality.* New York: Columbia University Press.

Sartre, J. P. (1963). *Existential Psychoanalysis,* trans. H. E. Barnes. Chicago: Regnery.

Scott, K. Y. (1991). *The Habit of Surviving.* New York: Ballantine.

Shaffer, P. (1977). *Equus.* New York: Avon.

Shaw, R. (1989). *The heartbeat of relationships: a heuristic investigation of interaction rhythms.* Unpublished doctoral dissertation, The Union Institute, Cincinnati, OH.

Smith, D. L. (1979). Phenomenological psychotherapy: a why and a how. In *Duquesne Studies in Phenomenological Psychology,* vol. 3, ed. A. Giorgi, R. Knowles, and D. L. Smith, pp. 32–48. Pittsburgh: Duquesne University Press.

Stead, C. (1940). *The Man Who Loved Children.* New York: Holt, Rinehart & Winston.

Steinbeck, J., and Ricketts, E. F. (1941). *Sea of Cortez.* New York: Viking.

Tracol, H. (1984). The taste for things that are true. *Parabola* 9(1): 22–25.

van den Berg, J. H. (1955). *The Phenomenological Approach to Psychiatry.* Springfield, IL: Thomas.

van der Hart, O. (1983). *Rituals in Psychotherapy*, trans. A. Pleit-Kulper. New York: Irvington.

van Dusen, W. (1973). The presence of spirits in madness. In *Exploring Madness*. ed. J. Fadiman and D. Kewman, pp. 118–134. San Francisco: Brooks/Cole.

Weems, L. X. (1975). The rhythm of black personality. In *African Philosophy: Assumptions and Paradigms for Research on Black Persons*, ed. L. M. King, pp. 54–79. Los Angeles: Fanon Research & Development Center.

Whitman, W. (1950). *Leaves of Grass*. New York: Harper.

Wittgenstein, L. (1953). *Philosophical Investigations*. New York: Macmillan.

# Credits

The author gratefully acknowledges permission to reprint material from the following:

# Credits

The author gratefully acknowledges permission to reprint
material from the following:

The critiques of Johannes Böhm, in "An Ecology of Investing"
Hand, by W. A. Spencer, 1964 and those edited The Open
Institute 1983, abstract. Translation, abstract, biography, et
al. 2006, copyright © 1973 "Klein Modular, s.a.k.

A Treatise on thinking: Debt Self, Communication, manuscript by C. S. Barry. Debt text, after 1st Harper, hard-book.
New copyright © 1981 Victory Industry.

Excerpts reprinted by R. M. Kills, Battle in Water's London,
Change Introduction of 1b. Copyright © 1961. In New York,
Times Publisher.

# Index